# Study Skills
## *for* Success

Lawrence J. Zwier

Glenn Mathes II

University of Michigan Press
Ann Arbor

# Contents

*List of Skills, by Lesson*   v

*List of Skills, by Type*   ix

*Introduction for Students and Teachers*   xi

## Part 1  Organizing Information

Lesson 1    Alphabetizing   3

Lesson 2    Making and Interpreting Time Lines   11

Lesson 3    Outlining   21

Lesson 4    Other Shortcuts for Organizing Information   29

Lesson 5    Review—Practicing Skills from Part 1   40

## Part 2  Reading and Interpreting Illustrated Information

Lesson 6    Reading and Interpreting Maps   51

Lesson 7    Reading and Interpreting Graphs   59

Lesson 8    Reading and Interpreting Charts and Tables   67

Lesson 9    Review—Practicing Skills from Part 2   76

## Part 3  Skills for Better Reading

Lesson 10    Determining the Main Idea   85

Lesson 11    Types of Writing on Assignments and Tests   99

Lesson 12    Scanning and Skimming   111

Lesson 13    Vocabulary Strategies   124

Lesson 14    Review—Practicing Skills from Part 3   137

## Part 4  Research Strategies

Lesson 15    Finding Information for Research    145
Lesson 16    Avoiding Plagiarism    155
Lesson 17    Review—Practicing Skills from Part 4    163
Lesson 18    Comprehensive Review—Practicing Skills
                    from All Parts          170

## Review

*Appendix A    State Abbreviations    175*
*Appendix B    Abbreviations for Geographical and
                      Directional Terms    176*
*Appendix C    Proofreading Symbols and Abbreviations    178*
*Appendix D    Temperature Conversion    181*
*Appendix E    Weights and Measures    182*

*Answer Key    186*

# List of Skills, by Lesson

| Part / Lesson | Title | Skills |
| --- | --- | --- |
| Part 1 | Organizing Information | |
| Lesson 1 | Alphabetizing | • Alphabetize words<br>• Alphabetize names of people |
| Lesson 2 | Making and Interpreting Time Lines | • Read horizontal and vertical time lines<br>• Interpret information provided in time lines<br>• Create a time line from given information |
| Lesson 3 | Outlining | • Determine first-, second-, and third-level ideas from a reading for outlining purposes<br>• State the characteristics of an outline<br>• Use written conventions of outlines<br>• Outline lecture notes and readings |
| Lesson 4 | Other Shortcuts for Organizing Information | • Create a graphic organizer<br>• Write marginal notes<br>• State the advantages and disadvantages of writing marginal notes<br>• Identify common abbreviations<br>• Abbreviate lecture notes<br>• Use note cards, sticky notes, and notebook tricks for organizing information |
| Lesson 5 | Review—Practicing Skills from Part 1 | |

| Part / Lesson | Title | Skills |
|---|---|---|
| Part 2 | Reading and Interpreting Illustrated Information | |
| Lesson 6 | Reading and Interpreting Maps | • Identify information provided by maps<br>• Read and interpret maps with keys<br>• Read and interpret readings with maps |
| Lesson 7 | Reading and Interpreting Graphs | • Identify and interpret bar graphs and line graphs<br>• Make predictions based on information presented in graphs<br>• Read and interpret graph legends |
| Lesson 8 | Reading and Interpreting Charts and Tables | • Identify and interpret pie charts<br>• Identify and interpret tables<br>• Identify information not provided by illustrated sources |
| Lesson 9 | Review—Practicing Skills from Part 2 | |
| Part 3 | Skills for Better Reading | |
| Lesson 10 | Determining the Main Idea | • Identify main ideas in reading passages<br>• Identify topics and topic statements<br>• Use the Umbrella Principle to determine which sentences support the main idea and which do not<br>• Identify main ideas through thesis statements or repetition of main points. |

| Part / Lesson | Title | Skills |
|---|---|---|
| Lesson 11 | Types of Writing on Assignments and Tests | • Identify appropriate levels of formality in various forms of writing<br>• Identify various genres of writing<br>• Use appropriate genres when responding to test questions |
| Lesson 12 | Scanning and Skimming | • Scan for information in books or on the Internet<br>• Skim various texts for details<br>• Identify and use key words when skimming for details |
| Lesson 13 | Vocabulary Strategies | • Understand that many words have various meanings and determining which meaning is appropriate to the context in which it is used<br>• Use a dictionary to determine the meanings of words<br>• Identify dictionary abbreviations for parts of speech<br>• Determine the meaning of a word based on context<br>• Use word parts to determine meaning<br>• Use notebooks, cards, and other systems to learn new vocabulary |
| Lesson 14 | Review—Practicing Skills from Part 3 | |

| Part / Lesson | Title | Skills |
|---|---|---|
| Part 4 | Research Strategies | |
| Lesson 15 | Finding Information for Research | • Identify sources of information available in libraries<br>• Perform searches by keyword, author, title, or Library of Congress number in online library catalogs<br>• Perform online searches to find information for research<br>• Identify the advantages and disadvantages of library versus online sources<br>• Determine whether to search library catalogs or online sources first when searching for information |
| Lesson 16 | Avoiding Plagiarism | • Identify examples of plagiarism<br>• Paraphrase information without plagiarizing<br>• Cite sources of information to avoid plagiarizing<br>• Identify statements of factual common knowledge |
| Lesson 17 | Review— Practicing Skills from Part 4 | |
| Lesson 18 | Comprehen- sive Review— Practicing Skills from All Parts | |

# List of Skills, by Type

| Skill | Lesson |
|---|---|
| Alphabetizing | 1,5,13,15 |
| Abbreviating | 4 |
| Chart Reading | 8,9 |
| Citing Sources | 16,17,18 |
| Dictionary Usage | 1,13 |
| Formality | 11 |
| Genres of Writing | 11 |
| Graphic Organizers | 4 |
| Graph Reading | 7 |
| Illustrated Information (Reading and Interpreting) | 6,7,8,9 |
| Key Words | 12 |
| Lecture Notes | 4 |
| Library Resources | 15,17,18 |
| Main Ideas | 10,14 |
| Map Reading | 6,9 |
| Marginal Notes | 4 |
| Notebooks | 4,13 |
| Note cards | 4, 13 |
| Online Resources (Using) | 15,17,18 |
| Organizing Information | 1,2,3,4,5,18 |
| Outlining | 3,18 |
| Paraphrasing | 16,17,18 |
| Plagiarism (Avoiding) | 16,17 |
| Reading Skills | 10,11,12,13,14 |

| Skill | Lesson |
|---|---|
| Research Strategies | 15,16,17,18 |
| Scanning | 12,14,18 |
| Skimming | 12,14,18 |
| Sticky Notes | 4 |
| Table Reading | 8,9 |
| Test Questions | 11 |
| Thesis Statements | 10 |
| Time Lines | 2,5,18 |
| Topics (Determining) | 10 |
| Topic Statements (Using) | 10 |
| Types of Writing (Determining) | 11,14 |
| Vocabulary Strategies | 13,14 |
| Umbrella Principle | 10 |

# Introduction for Students and Teachers

This book teaches and reviews some basic study strategies and skills that can help students succeed in their last years of high school or in college. It was written with non-native speakers of English in mind, although native speakers of English will find it useful as well. The language of explanation and practice is appropriate for students whose English proficiency is in the intermediate to high-intermediate range.

Pages vii–xii provide an inventory of important study skills and a list of lessons that address each skill. Use this correlation table to see how certain concepts are recycled throughout the book. For example, the skill of distinguishing between main ideas and subsidiary ideas is important in Lesson 3 (Outlining) as well as in Lesson 10 (Determining the Main Idea).

Some of the skills taught in this book, such as alphabetizing, are very mechanical and have a definite "correct" outcome. Others, such as researching a topic, require more thought and inventiveness. In both cases—and in many others in between—we offer advice and practice for developing the skills. **Critical thinking** is exercised as students evaluate the usefulness of certain strategies. **Inductive learning** is encouraged by exercises that ask students to recognize patterns in common academic tools like outlines, notes, and Internet searches.

Skills are built by practicing them. This book emphasizes production by the students and peer discussion of their products. Each lesson contains a little bit of advice and a lot of exercises. A review lesson appears at the end of each part, and Lesson 18 is a review of the major skills taught throughout the book.

Strategy boxes contain advice about specific study skills, and Tip boxes offer advice on various aspects of study skill success.

We hope that you enjoy working with this book and that it becomes one of your most useful tools in building academic success.

# PART 1

# Organizing Information

# Alphabetizing

**Alphabetizing** is the process of ordering items according to their first letters (A, B, C, D, etc.). Alphabetizing is used for putting books in order in libraries, for putting CDs in order at music stores, and for putting names in order in phone books.

Where else can you find items that are alphabetized?

_____

_____

_____

_____

We alphabetize to make information easy to find, for ourselves and others.

You will use alphabetizing to find information at a library, to put vocabulary words and names in order for studying, and to list your sources in research papers.

For what other purposes do you think you can use alphabetizing?

_____

_____

_____

_____

# ◎ How to Alphabetize Words

1. Look at the first letters of the words given.

2. Put the words in order according to their first letters (A, B, C, etc.).

3. If any words have the same first letter, use the second letters of the words to alphabetize. For example, *car* would be alphabetized before *core.*

4. If the second letters are the same, use the third letters, then fourth letters, etc., until you can put the words in order. So, *cap* would be alphabetized before *car,* which would be alphabetized before *cat.*

**Example**

You need to study some terms for a psychology class. You want to alphabetize these terms so you can reference them later. Three of the terms are:

> super ego
> id
> ego

You would alphabetize the terms in the following order:

> **e**go
> **i**d
> **s**uper ego

because **e** comes before **i** in the alphabet and **s** comes after **i** in the alphabet. If the word has more than one word, you should use the first word when alphabetizing.

## EXERCISE 1

Look at the following sets of terms taken from various textbooks. Write numbers in the space next to each term to show the order in which they should be alphabetized. The first set has been done for you.

| | | | |
|---|---|---|---|
| quark | 2 | attack | ____ |
| nova | 1 | blitzkrieg | ____ |
| supernova | 3 | surrender | ____ |
| worm hole | 4 | invasion | ____ |
| | | | |
| quadrant | ____ | solution | ____ |
| quadrilateral | ____ | element | ____ |
| parallelogram | ____ | atom | ____ |
| | | mixture | ____ |
| pianissimo | ____ | nucleus | ____ |
| staccato | ____ | | |
| pizzicato | ____ | | |
| allegro | ____ | | |

## EXERCISE 2

Practice by alphabetizing these words found in a chapter of a social studies textbook about the early American colonies. The first word has been done for you.

| | |
|---|---|
| pilgrim | 1. colony |
| colony | 2. _____ |
| freedom | 3. _____ |
| settlement | 4. _____ |
| persecution | 5. _____ |
| settlers | 6. _____ |

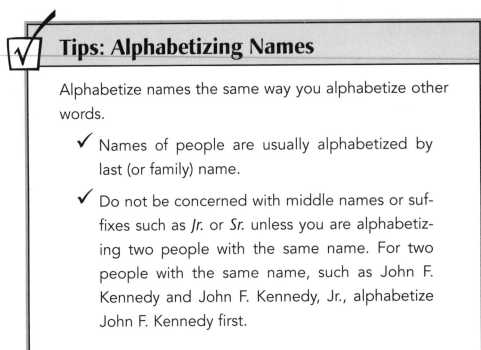

## Tips: Alphabetizing Names

Alphabetize names the same way you alphabetize other words.

✓ Names of people are usually alphabetized by last (or family) name.

✓ Do not be concerned with middle names or suffixes such as *Jr.* or *Sr.* unless you are alphabetizing two people with the same name. For two people with the same name, such as John F. Kennedy and John F. Kennedy, Jr., alphabetize John F. Kennedy first.

## EXERCISE 3

*Practice by alphabetizing the names of these famous civil rights activists. The first one has been done for you.*

| | |
|---|---|
| Martin Luther King, Jr. | 1. César Chávez |
| Rosa Parks | 2. _____ |
| Jesse Jackson | 3. _____ |
| Medgar Evers | 4. _____ |
| César Chávez | 5. _____ |

## ▼ Alphabetizing Words from Reading Passages for Study Purposes

You may encounter unfamiliar or difficult words in your reading. To learn and remember these words more effectively, organize them in a list and write the definitions next to them.

*Read this passage that could be found in a science textbook. Important terms have been underlined.*

In 1926, Robert Goddard launched the first liquid-fuel rocket in the United States. However, it wasn't until 1957 that the first <u>satellite</u> was launched into <u>orbit</u> by the Soviet Union. In 1959, Yuri Gagarin, a Russian <u>cosmonaut</u>, became the first human being to go into space and orbit Earth. In the same year, the Russians also launched the first <u>interplanetary probe</u> to Venus. The U.S. sent its first <u>astronaut</u>, Alan B. Shepard, into space in 1961. Shepard's trip was a <u>suborbital</u> trip. A year later, astronaut John Herschel Glenn, Jr., became the first U.S. astronaut to orbit Earth, three years after Gagarin. The Russian space program achieved another first by sending Valentina Vladimirovna Tereshkova into orbit in 1963. Tereshkova was a female cosmonaut and was thus the first woman to go into space. The Russians and Americans continued the <u>space race</u> throughout the 1960s, until the U.S. landed the first humans on another body in orbit in 1969. Neil Armstrong and Edwin "Buzz" Aldrin, U.S. astronauts in the Apollo 11 mission, became the first humans to walk on the Moon in July 1969.

## EXERCISE 4

*Now, alphabetize the underlined terms in the passage. After alphabetizing the terms, write the meaning of the words based on what you read in the passage.*

1.


2.


3.


4.


5.


6.

7.

## ▼ Alphabetizing Names from Reading Passages for Study Purposes

You may also encounter unfamiliar names in your reading. To remember and study these names, organize them in a list, and write important information about these people.

*Using the same passage about the space race, circle all of the names of people.*

In 1926, Robert Goddard launched the first liquid-fuel rocket in the United States. However, it wasn't until 1957 that the first satellite was launched into orbit by the Soviet Union. In 1959, Yuri Gagarin, a Russian cosmonaut, became the first human being to go into space and orbit

Earth. In the same year, the Russians also launched the first interplanetary probe to Venus. The U.S. sent its first astronaut, Alan B. Shepard, into space in 1961. Shepard's trip was a suborbital trip. A year later, astronaut John Herschel Glenn, Jr., became the first U.S. astronaut to orbit Earth, three years after Gagarin. The Russian space program achieved another first by sending Valentina Vladimirovna Tereshkova into orbit in 1963. Tereshkova was a female cosmonaut and was thus the first woman to go into space. The Russians and Americans continued the space race throughout the 1960s, until the U.S. landed the first humans on another body in orbit in 1969. Neil Armstrong and Edwin "Buzz" Aldrin, U.S. astronauts in the Apollo 11 mission, became the first humans to walk on the Moon in July 1969.

## EXERCISE 5

*Now, alphabetize all of the names you found in the passage, and write why they are famous next to their names.*

# Making and Interpreting Time Lines

A **time line** is a list of events in the order in which they occurred. So these events can easily be seen, they are placed on a line. Time lines can be written horizontally:

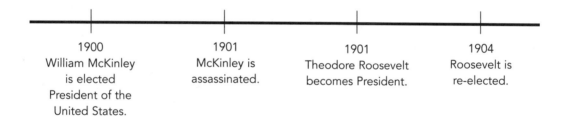

| 1900 | 1901 | 1901 | 1904 |
|---|---|---|---|
| William McKinley is elected President of the United States. | McKinley is assassinated. | Theodore Roosevelt becomes President. | Roosevelt is re-elected. |

The earliest event is on the left end of the line. The most recent event is on the right.

Time lines can also be written vertically. Then, the earliest event is at the top of the line. The most recent event is at the bottom of the line.

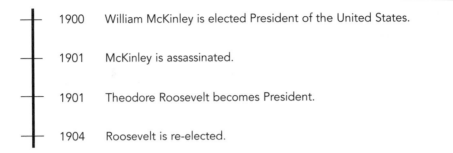

| | 1900 | William McKinley is elected President of the United States. |
| | 1901 | McKinley is assassinated. |
| | 1901 | Theodore Roosevelt becomes President. |
| | 1904 | Roosevelt is re-elected. |

Time lines can be organized by any unit of time (years, months, hours, etc.). Notice that in both time lines, two events happened in 1901. Since McKinley was assassinated before Roosevelt could become President, that event is listed first.

In what classes could you use time lines?

_____     _____

_____     _____

## EXERCISE 1

*Look at this time line, and answer the questions that follow.*

### The Life of John F. Kennedy

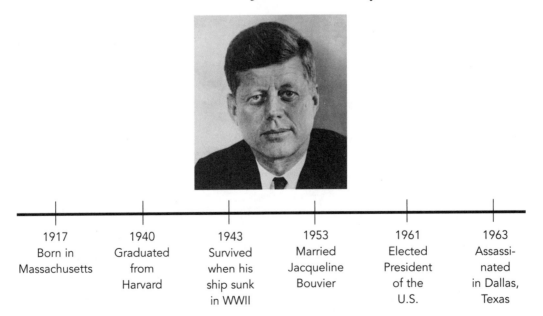

| 1917 | 1940 | 1943 | 1953 | 1961 | 1963 |
|------|------|------|------|------|------|
| Born in Massachusetts | Graduated from Harvard | Survived when his ship sunk in WWII | Married Jacqueline Bouvier | Elected President of the U.S. | Assassinated in Dallas, Texas |

1. What is the title of this time line?

   _____

2. What happened first on this time line? When did it happen?

   _____

3. What happened last on this time line? When did it happen?

   _____

4. When was Kennedy elected President of the United States?

   _____

5. When was he killed?

   _____

√ **Tips: Interpreting Time Lines**

   ✓ Look at the title to understand the content of the time line.

   ✓ Look at the first and last years to know how much time is covered on the time line.

   ✓ Look at each date and event.

## EXERCISE 2

*Make a time line of your life. Start by organizing the important events in your life.*

1. Year and place of birth _____

2. Year you started elementary school _____

3. Year you started middle school _____

4. Year you started high school _____

5. Other important events _____

_____

*Title your time line. Then, write in all the dates and events you listed.*

Title: _____

**EXERCISE 3**

*Now exchange the time line of your life with someone else in the class. Answer the following questions based on that person's time line.*

1. Whose time line are you reading?

   _____

2. What is the title of the time line?

   _____

3. When was the person born? _____

4. Where was the person born? _____

5. When did (s)he start elementary school? _____

6. When did (s)he start middle school?_____

7. When did (s)he start high school?_____

8. What other events are listed on the time line?

   _____

*Now, put your answers into a short paragraph about that person's life.*

_____

_____

_____

_____

_____

_____

_____

_____

## ▼ Reading a Time Line

Some books, such as history textbooks or biographies, present information in time lines. Reading this information will make it easier for you to understand the reading passages in those books.

### √ Tip: Constructing a Time Line

Many time lines place events far away from each other if a large amount of time passed between events. When making your own time lines, you may want to do the same thing to help you see the amount of time between events more easily.

## EXERCISE 4

*Look at the following time line. Answer the questions that follow.*

**States Admitted to the Union since 1890**

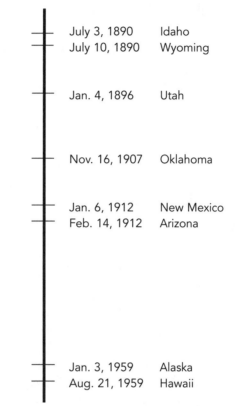

July 3, 1890 — Idaho
July 10, 1890 — Wyoming

Jan. 4, 1896 — Utah

Nov. 16, 1907 — Oklahoma

Jan. 6, 1912 — New Mexico
Feb. 14, 1912 — Arizona

Jan. 3, 1959 — Alaska
Aug. 21, 1959 — Hawaii

1. How many states have been admitted to the United States since 1890? _____

2. Which state was the last one to be admitted to the United States? _____

3. When was the last state admitted to the United States, according to the time line? _____

4. How many states were admitted in 1890? _____

5. How many states were admitted in 1900? _____

6. How many states were admitted in 1959? _____

7. How many years passed between Arizona becoming a state and Alaska becoming a state?   _____

8. Which states are close together on the time line?

   _____

9. Why are those states close together?

   _____

10. Why is there a large space between Arizona and Alaska becoming states?

   _____

   _____

## ▼ Making a Time Line from Given Information

You may be given information in a book, lecture, or notes that you can put into a time line for study purposes.

### EXERCISE 5

*Suppose you are studying world history. Put the following information about Russia (formerly known as the Soviet Union) during World War II into the time line.*

1945    The Soviet Union's leader Joseph Stalin met with British and American leaders to discuss how to divide Europe after the war.

1943    German troops at Stalingrad surrender.

1941   The German army invaded the Soviet Union without warning.

1939   The Soviet Union agreed to split Poland with Germany after Germany invaded Poland and began World War II.

1944   The Soviet Union drove the German army from Pskov, the last large Russian city.

**Important Soviet Events during World War II**

1939

1940

1941

1942

1943

1944

1945

**EXERCISE 6**

*Answer the following questions about the time line you have created.*

1. What event happened first on the time line?_____

   _____

2. When did that event happen? _____

3. When did the last event on the time line occur? _____

4. Looking at the dates on the time line, between what
   years did World War II occur? _____

5. When did the Soviet army push the German army out
   of the last large Russian city? _____

6. Was the Soviet Union at war with Germany during all
   of World War II? _____

7. Explain your answer to question 6.

   _____

   _____

   _____

# Outlining

Outlining is a way of listing the main points of a reading or lecture. This list shows relationships among the main points—especially between large ideas and the smaller ideas within them.

## ▼ Outlining Can Be Used to List the Main Ideas in a Reading

Teachers sometimes assign you to outline a reading to show that you can distinguish main points from supporting details. Also, some students like to study this way—outlining the things they read to make sure they've got it right.

Notice the highlighted items in the reading and how they can be organized into an outline.

| Reading | Outline |
|---|---|
| Railroad owners became very rich in the mid-nineteenth century because of various governmental and societal factors. To encourage the development of railroads, the federal government rewarded railroad companies with huge tracts of free land, far more than they needed to lay their track. The government also paid for many of the bridges and tunnels the railroad men need. Add to these benefits the contracts for railroads to deliver government mail, to transport soldiers and their materiel, and to deliver various other services, and you see a vast network of federal support for the railroads.<br><br>Meanwhile, the spread of the American population ensured that the railroads would get rich. By the 1840s, when California joined the Union, the United States had become a bi-coastal nation. The famous wagon-train treks through the Great Plains were hazardous and trying. A population eager to move west was eager to pay well for the safety and speed the railroads were selling. As the network of track reached into mining territory, lumber towns, and the grain belts of the Midwest, those who had already traveled west were eager to pay the railroads to transport raw materials to the depot cities of Chicago, Kansas City, and even the great old port cities of the East Coast. | Reasons for prosperity of railroads<br><br>I. Governmental reasons<br><br>  A. Free land<br><br>  B. Gov't paid for bridges & tunnels<br><br>  C. Gov't contracts to railroads<br><br>    1. deliver mail<br><br>    2. transport soldiers<br><br>    3. deliver other services<br><br>II. Societal reasons<br><br>  A. "bi-coastal nation"<br><br>  B. train travel preferred over slower, more dangerous wagon trains<br><br>  C. RRs preferred for freight |

first-level ideas

second-level ideas

third-level ideas

**EXERCISE 1**

*Highlight the first-, second-, and third-level ideas in the following reading,
Use the system of boxes, ovals, and underlining from the previous example.*

## *Tax Policy*

The main use of federal tax policy is to raise money for the government. However, it is also a tool for influencing people's spending behavior, an instrument of industrial strategy, a means of advancing moral causes, and more.

For a perfect example of the first, look at the charitable-deduction rule in American tax law. To encourage charitable giving, we create a tax incentive for it. The same goes for the mortgage interest deduction. To encourage people to buy their own homes—a good way of developing roots in the community—the government gives a credit for the interest paid in doing so.

A perfect example of the tax law as an instrument of industrial policy is the tax credit given to farmers who grow corn for alcohol (to be mixed with gasoline). Tax law encourages the development of this ethanol industry. And the moral side of tax law can be seen in the battle over federal funding of stem-cell research. Those in the administration who find such research immoral make it impossible to use U.S. tax dollars to pursue it. This is a lot easier than declaring the practice itself wrong.

**EXERCISE 2**

*Using the ideas you highlighted in Exercise 1, fill in the blanks in the out-line. First-level points I and II have been filled in for you, as have parts of III and IV.*

## The Use of U. S. Tax Policy

I. Raise money for the government


II. Influence spending behavior

    a. _____

    b. _____


III. _____ (e.g., tax credits for ethanol)


IV. _____ (e.g., stem-cell research)

Notice that in first-level ideas III and IV, there are no separate lines for second-level ideas. That's because, in each case, the reading gives only one. As you can see in the sample, you can write this one piece of support on the same line as the first-level idea (usually in parentheses with *e.g.*). If there were two or more, they'd be listed on separate lines and more clearly identified as second-level ideas.

Can you think of some other ways outlining is used?

_____   _____

## EXERCISE 3: CRITICAL THINKING

*What makes one outline better than another? What characteristics should a good outline have? Complete this list as well as you can.*

### Characteristics of a Good Outline

1. Only main points go in an outline.

2. Points are not whole sentences.

3. _____

4. _____

5. _____

6. _____

7. _____

8. _____

## ◎ Advice for Outlining a Lecture or a Reading

1. Look at what you will outline—your lecture notes, a reading, a film, etc.

2. Identify main ideas at different levels. Highlight them in different colors or with different symbols.

3. For each main idea, a section of your outline will look like this:

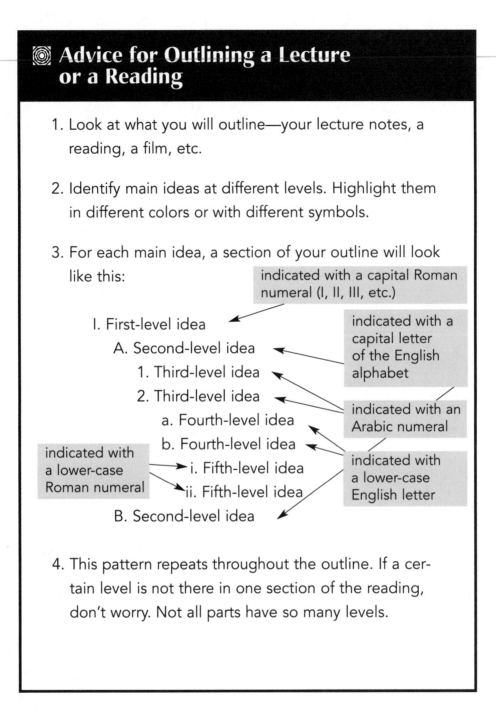

indicated with a capital Roman numeral (I, II, III, etc.)

I. First-level idea

indicated with a capital letter of the English alphabet

  A. Second-level idea

    1. Third-level idea

indicated with an Arabic numeral

    2. Third-level idea

      a. Fourth-level idea

indicated with a lower-case English letter

      b. Fourth-level idea

indicated with a lower-case Roman numeral

        i. Fifth-level idea

        ii. Fifth-level idea

  B. Second-level idea

4. This pattern repeats throughout the outline. If a certain level is not there in one section of the reading, don't worry. Not all parts have so many levels.

## ▼ Outlining Something You Plan to Say or Write

Many speakers and writers use outlines as a way of organizing speeches, presentations, or reports.

### EXERCISE 4

*Pretend you have to give a five-minute speech titled, "Is It Safe to Drink the Water?" Organize the points for your speech by writing an outline. Rearrange the information in the list, delete some because it doesn't fit, or look up new information to fill gaps.*

- underground water picks up different pollutants from above-ground water—oil, gas, manure, sewage, chemicals
- as water flows through sand or stone, some impurities are filtered out
- bad to mix sewage systems from homes with storm runoff
- filters can be installed in homes
- public water sources should be inspected
- factories: what are they putting into water?
- living bacteria or algae can make you sick
- waste from animals or humans

### ✓ Tips: Outlining

✓ The idea of a whole piece should be a **title**, not part of your outline.

✓ Your first try at an outline will not be perfect. Make changes if necessary.

✓ Most outlines have three or four levels. Most do not go as far as five levels. If you think you need a sixth or seventh level, reconsider. You may have too many points, or you may have grouped them wrongly.

## ▼ Outlining Can Be Used to Organize Notes from a Lecture or Conversation

The notes you take while people are speaking may be hard to read or confusing. This is partly because you had to write very quickly. Also, speakers don't always organize their ideas clearly. Ideas that belong together may be scattered through different parts of the lecture or conversation. When you outline your notes later, you put them in a form that's easier to understand.

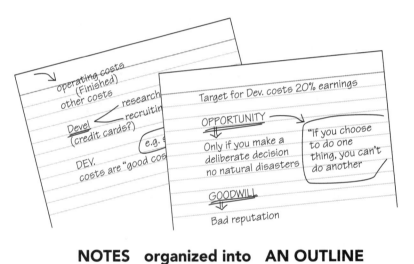

**NOTES organized into AN OUTLINE**

Non-Operating Costs

I. Development
   A. Involves future research & staff
   B. Are "good costs"

II. Opportunity Costs
   A. Result from a deliberate decision
   B. Not doing something means not making money

III. Goodwill costs—"a bad reputation"

# Other Shortcuts for Organizing Information

---

## ▼ Graphic Organizers/Mind Maps

---

Some people think outlines are too limited and restrictive. They prefer a slightly different method called the graphic organizer or mind map.

Like an outline, the graphic organizer shows relationships among ideas in a lecture or reading. Take another look at the first reading from Lesson 3 (about railroads) and then at the graphic organizer that follows it.

### *Reading*

Railroad owners became very rich in the mid-nineteenth century because of various governmental and societal factors. To encourage the development of railroads, the federal government rewarded railroad companies with huge tracts of free land, far more than they needed to lay their track. The government also paid for many of the bridges and tunnels the railroad men needed. Add to these benefits the contracts for railroads to deliver government mail, to transport soldiers and their materiel, and to deliver various other

<u>services</u>, and you see a vast network of federal support for the railroads.

Meanwhile, the spread of the American population ensured that the railroads would get rich. By the 1840s, when California joined the Union, the United States had become a bi-coastal nation. The famous wagon-train treks through the Great Plains were hazardous and trying. A population eager to move west was eager to pay well for the safety and speed the railroads were selling. As the network of track reached into mining territory, lumber towns, and the grain belts of the Midwest, those who had already traveled west were eager to pay the railroads to transport raw materials to the depot cities of Chicago, Kansas City, and even the great old port cities of the East Coast.

Now, see how the same material could be organized in a graphic organizer.

## Graphic Organizer

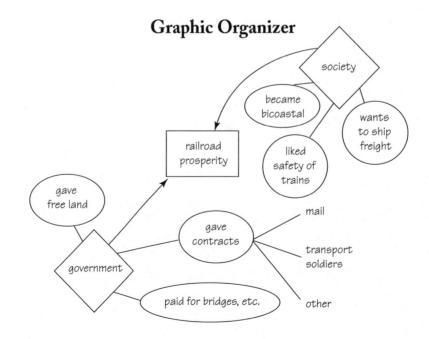

A graphic organizer looks a lot different from an outline, but it can be easier for some people to remember.

## ▼ Marginal Notes

A margin is an empty space, usually at the sides of a reading. If you have your own copy of the reading—a book that you own, a handout that you may keep, etc.—marginal notes can be very convenient.

Notice this piece of writing in which the student has written marginal notes.

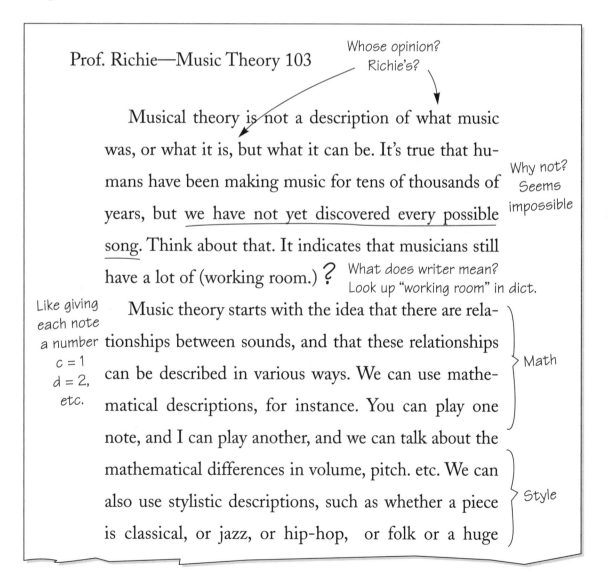

Prof. Richie—Music Theory 103

*Whose opinion?*
*Richie's?*

Musical theory is not a description of what music was, or what it is, but what it can be. It's true that humans have been making music for tens of thousands of years, but we have not yet discovered every possible song. Think about that. It indicates that musicians still have a lot of (working room.) **?**

*Why not?*
*Seems impossible*

*What does writer mean?*
*Look up "working room" in dict.*

*Like giving each note a number*
*c = 1*
*d = 2,*
*etc.*

Music theory starts with the idea that there are relationships between sounds, and that these relationships can be described in various ways. We can use mathematical descriptions, for instance. You can play one note, and I can play another, and we can talk about the mathematical differences in volume, pitch. etc. We can also use stylistic descriptions, such as whether a piece is classical, or jazz, or hip-hop, or folk or a huge

*Math*

*Style*

This student was working with a photocopy of notes handed out in class, so writing in the margins of the sheet was perfectly all right.

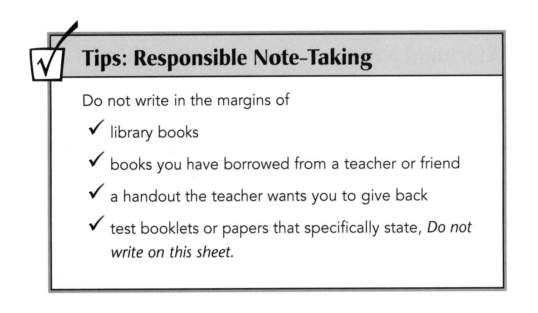

**Tips: Responsible Note-Taking**

Do not write in the margins of

✓ library books

✓ books you have borrowed from a teacher or friend

✓ a handout the teacher wants you to give back

✓ test booklets or papers that specifically state, *Do not write on this sheet.*

By using marginal notes, the note-taker can draw arrows, circle things, and otherwise avoid repeating words from the text. This saves *quite a bit* of time.

## EXERCISE 1: CRITICAL THINKING

*Marginal notes are not always the best way of taking notes. What makes marginal notes effective? In what ways are they ineffective? Fill out this table to list the good and bad points of using marginal notes.*

| Advantages of Using Marginal Notes | Disadvantages of Using Marginal Notes |
| --- | --- |
| Don't have to re-write words that are already printed<br><br>Can use arrows | Sometimes margins are thin and you can't write much |

**EXERCISE 2**

*Here is a handout from a social studies class. Write in marginal notes that would help you understand and remember the material. (Answers will vary; one sample is given in the Answer Key.)*

### The Trail of Tears

To the American government, it became obvious after the Louisiana Purchase (1803) that the "Indian Problem" in the Southeast should involve shipping Indians West. These included the Cherokees (who call themselves the Ani Yun Wiya).

The Cherokees had developed a civilization that whites had to respect. Their system of Civil Law was advanced, and they had a written language—in their own, unique characters, not just an English-letter transliteration.

Once gold was discovered under Cherokee land in Georgia, the federal Indian Removal Act of 1830 sealed the Cherokees' fate.

About 16,000 Cherokees, divided into 16 units, were assembled under Andrew Jackson's generals and headed west, toward what is now Oklahoma. Some traveled on the Arkansas River, which was full of debris and ice from spring melt-off. Others traveled by land across roadless territory with few clean sources of water. Altogether about 8,000 Cherokees died along what has become known as the Trail of Tears.

# ▼ Abbreviations

An **abbreviation** is a shortened way of writing something: *CD* is short for *compact disc.* *U.S.* is short for the *United States.* Abbreviations can help you take notes more quickly and set more information down on paper. The trick is to have a system so you can understand your abbreviations after you write them.

## ▽ COMMON ABBREVIATIONS

Certain abbreviations are widely used, as are some shortcuts for replacing words with symbols. Here are some examples that will help your own note-taking and can help you understand other people's notes.

| Abbreviation | Meaning | Example |
|---|---|---|
| *e.g.* | for example | *types of housing, **e.g.**, apartments, trailers, houses* |
| *vs.* | against | *in this debate, it's the environmentalists **vs.** builders* |
| *cf.* | refer to | Early works (***cf.** Jones 1937*) tried to show . . . . |
| = | equals; is the same as | *democracy = rule by people* |
| ≠ | does not equal; is not the same as | *high salary ≠ high social status* |
| → | leads to; causes | *heat → expansion* |

## EXERCISE 3

*Here are some other common abbreviations. Match the word or phrase in the left column with the best abbreviation from the right column. Write the letter in the blank. Compare your answers with a partner's.*

| Full form | Abbreviation |
|---|---|
| 1. _____ therefore | a. 3 dist syst |
| 2. _____ something | b. ∴ |
| 3. _____ more than | c. Ø |
| 4. _____ according to Johnson | d. ◅ |
| 5. _____ United Nations | e. ca.; approx. |
| 6. _____ about; approximately | f. johnson: |
| 7. _____ forbidden | g. sthg |
| 8. _____ later on | h. > |
| 9. _____ three distribution systems | i. UN |

## EXERCISE 4

*What characteristics do abbreviations have? Add to the following list.*

1. long words get chopped off ("dist sys")

2. use initials

3. _____

4. _____

5. _____

6. _____

## EXERCISE 5

*Some lecture notes written out in full form—with no abbreviations— follow. For each note, abbreviate one or more items. Use your own system, but make sure you would understand your shortened notes later. Compare your notes with those of a partner. Do you notice any patterns used by you, your partner, or both?*

| Notes in Full Form | Your Abbreviation |
|---|---|
| Shakespeare's romantic plays are perfect examples of the English Renaissance. | |
| A package sent via the National Postal Service costs three cents per pound less than the next-cheapest service. | |
| Sir Nigel Watson fought Madame Gemma Stykes for leadership of the Worker's Party. | |
| Upper respiratory infections become common in the winter not because of cold but because more people are gathered indoors for a long time. | |

## ▼ Other Tips for Organization

### ▽ NOTE CARDS

There are times when you might write your notes on cards instead of paper. Note cards are especially helpful if you are giving a speech. Note cards allow you to:

- try different ways of organizing facts
- easily skip something if you are running short on time
- add new information at the last minute
- give you something to hold onto while you are nervous in front of your class

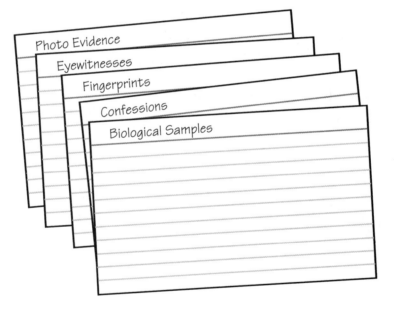

## √ Tips: Taking Notes

### *Sticky Notes:*

✓ If you need more room for marginal notes, use "sticky notes" and place them at the proper place on a text.

✓ Used different-colored sticky notes for different purposes: yellow for statistics, blue for important quotes, etc.

### *Notebook Tricks:*

✓ In your notebooks, take notes only on the left page of an open spread. Then, when it comes time to outline them, you'll have open space right where you need it.

✓ If you have your own system of abbreviations that might be hard to remember, write it on the inside cover of your notebook and refer to it when you need to.

# Review–Practicing Skills from Part 1

In Lessons 1–4, you learned how to alphabetize, how to create a time line, how to outline, and how to use other shortcuts for organizing information. You will now have a chance to practice what you've learned.

*First, read the following passage on the Founders of the United States. Then, practice organizing the information from the reading in order to prepare an oral report.*

### *The Founders*

It is generally accepted that the country that became the United States of America was formed by a small group referred to as the Founders. The most famous and important Founders were George Washington, Thomas Jefferson, Benjamin Franklin, John Adams, James Madison, James Monroe, Alexander Hamilton, and Aaron Burr. This group, along with others, helped the United States become the first country to be created by revolution without any major incident of bloodshed following the revolution (until the U.S.

Civil War, about 80 years later). They helped unite a group of separate states in order to create the country that would become a long-standing model for the republican form of government.

During the 1760s and 1770s, while America was a group of colonies owned by Great Britain, the colonies began to become angry. The British Parliament passed a series of taxes that the colonists felt were unfair. However, the colonists were unable to protest these acts because they had no one representing them in Parliament. The colonists' anger at being taxed without being able to vote on the taxes caused them to rebel against Great Britain.

In 1774, the First Continental Congress met to issue a list of complaints to the King of England. The Congress included many of the Founders. In 1775, the Revolutionary War began. General George Washington was put in charge of the colonist troops, which were composed of disorganized and undisciplined soldiers from various colonies. Washington created a group of officers and introduced discipline to these untrained men. A year later, in 1776, having seen no change in England's position, Thomas Jefferson was charged with drafting the Declaration of Independence. This document declared that the colonies were no longer a part of Great Britain.

Benjamin Franklin, a printer, philosopher, scientist, and famous American in both the colonies and Europe, was sent to France to ask for money, ships, and support for the colonies. After long negotiations, Franklin and his assistants managed to get help from the French. The French had wanted to see if the colonists could possibly defeat the British. As Washington continued to fight despite limited money and supplies, the French began to believe that the colonists had a chance at victory and offered their support.

War continued until 1781, when the British General Cornwallis surrendered at Yorktown. The colonies became the United States of America. However, the states were anything but united. Under the Articles of Confederation drafted by the Continental Congress in 1777, the loose union of states was held together by a weak central government. These articles were replaced by the U.S. Constitution in 1789, after a great deal of debate. The Founders had different views on how the new country's government should be formed, and often fought over their ideas and interests.

However, everyone agreed that a leader should be chosen to unite the states. Benjamin Franklin suggested that the hero of the Revolution could help unite the country, and George Washington was elected the first President of the United States under the new Constitution in 1789.

Now that the country had obtained its independence, it was faced with the task of forming a stable government. One group of Founders called the Federalists (consisting of such great leaders as James Madison and Alexander Hamilton) wanted a strong central government. Others feared a strong government, like the British government they just fought, and wanted states' rights. Thomas Jefferson would later form the Democratic-Republican party in opposition to the Federalists. Although the Founders never imagined the idea of political parties, the creation of these first two parties helped shape the country forever.

The new country was not given credit by international banks because it was unable to pay back its wartime loans. Alexander Hamilton, Washington's Secretary of the Treasury, created a plan for the central government to take over the states' wartime debts. If this plan were accepted by the Congress, it would form a strong central government. Madison was against the plan since his state, Virginia, had already paid most of its debts. However, Jefferson helped make a deal between Madison and Hamilton. Hamilton's plan was adopted, and Madison and Jefferson's state,

Virginia, along with a small part of Maryland, became the site of the new capital (later named Washington, DC).

As a stronger federal government began to form, Madison continued to worry about abuses of power by the government. Because of his involvement with the Constitution and the Bill of Rights, Madison is called "the father of the Constitution." In 1791 the Bill of Rights was added to the Constitution—ten amendments that would protect Americans' individual rights.

Although these Founders resolved most of their differences by arguing and negotiating, Hamilton was eventually shot and killed in a duel by Aaron Burr, a political enemy and Vice-President of the U.S. at the time. Otherwise, they generally made deals and made the decisions that would form the government of the United States. Following Washington (1789–1797*) as president were Adams (1797–1801*), Jefferson (1801–1809*), Madison (1809–1817*), and Monroe (1817–1825*) who made important decisions for the future of the federal government of the United States.

*Indicates years served as president

## EXERCISE 1: ALPHABETIZING

*Several Founders were listed in the previous reading. Write the names of all Founders listed. Then, alphabetize the names in order.*

**Names of the Founders:**

**Alphabetical List:**

## EXERCISE 2: TIME LINE

*Create a time line of the events listed in the reading. Don't forget to include the beginning and end of the Revolutionary War and the years that the Founders served as presidents of the United States.*

## EXERCISE 3: OUTLINING

*Now that you have begun to organize the information from the reading, put the information into an outline or mind map in the space given here. You may want to organize the names of the Founders in alphabetical order, or you may want to organize the events in chronological order. Look at your list of Founders in Exercise 1 and your timeline in Exercise 2 to decide how to organize your outline or mind map. At this time, you may also want to go back to the reading and write notes in the margins.*

## EXERCISE 4: NOTES

*Next, imagine that you need to prepare and present an oral report to your class on the Founders. Use note cards to prepare your report. Use abbreviations in your notes in order to include as much information as possible.*

# PART 2

# Reading and Interpreting Illustrated Information

# Reading and Interpreting Maps

There is an old expression that says, "A picture is worth a thousand words." This expression is true when we look at illustrated information such as maps.

Maps usually provide a great deal of information in the form of a picture of an area.

They can give you information on:

- the size and shape of an area (geographical map)
- the landscape, physical features, roads, and buildings of an area (topographical map)
- the roads of an area (road map)
- the people of an area (population map)
- the economic characteristics of an area
- and other information on an area

You may encounter maps in classes on history, geography, sociology, or other subjects.

The first key to reading a map is to determine what **area** and **subject matter** the map shows. You can usually determine this by looking at **the title of the map**.

## EXERCISE 1

*Look at Map 1 and answer the questions.*

1. What is the title of the map?

_____

2. What area does the map show?

_____

3. What subject does the map describe?

_____

## Map 1: The Continental United States

The map shows the continental United States. It consists of 48 of the 50 states (Alaska and Hawaii are not included). This map simply shows the shape of the United States and its continental states. It does not give any information on the landscape or the people who live there.

## ▼ Reading and Interpreting Maps with Keys

**EXERCISE 2**

*Now, look at Map 2, and answer the questions.*

### Map 2: U.S. Population Percent Change, 1990–2000

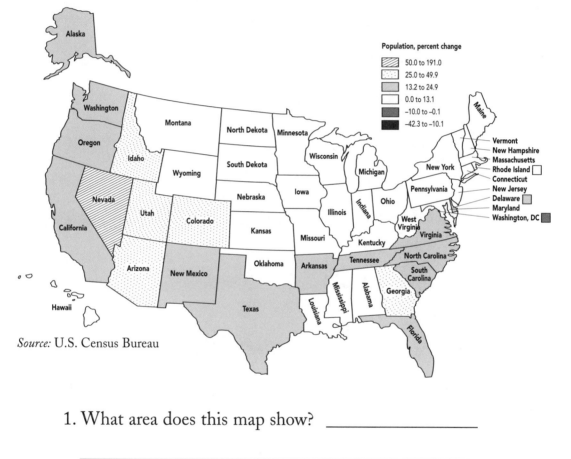

*Source:* U.S. Census Bureau

1. What area does this map show? _____

   _____

2. What information does it provide? _____

   _____

3. What does the color-coded key above the map show?

   _____

4. Who created this map? _____

   _____

**EXERCISE 3**

*Now answer these questions about specific information Map 2 provides.*

1. Which state had the largest population growth from 1990 to 2000?

   a. Arizona

   b. Nevada

   c. Georgia

   d. all of the above

2. Which of the following states had 25.0 percent to 49.9 percent growth from 1990 to 2000?

   a. Arizona

   b. Nevada

   c. Rhode Island

3. Which of the following states had no change or very little change in population from 1990 to 2000?

   a. West Virginia

   b. North Dakota

   c. Pennsylvania

   d. all of the above

4. Which area had the largest negative population change from 1990 to 2000?

    a. West Virginia

    b. Iowa

    c. Washington, DC

    d. all of the above

5. If an area had negative population change, which of the following do you think is true?

    a. Many people moved away from the area.

    b. Many people moved to the area.

    c. Many people in the area had children.

---

## √ Tip: Taking Tests

When taking tests or practice tests, you will sometimes see *all of the above* or *none of the above* as an answer. If one of the answers can be eliminated, you can rule out *all of the above* or *none of the above* and give yourself fewer answers to choose from.

## ▼ Reading and Interpreting Information from Maps and Readings

Sometimes you will be given a reading passage and a map. You can find quite a bit of information by reading and interpreting both.

---

### √ Tips: Reading Maps

Places on maps are often written in different ways. On some maps, some or all place names might be written in capital letters. On other maps, place names may be written with capital and lower-case letters. However, there are some things that most maps have in common:

✓ The larger the place, the larger its name will be written. The name of a city will be written larger than the name of a village. The name of a state, province, or prefecture will be written larger than the name of a city.

✓ A capital city will usually be marked with a star.

✓ The names of islands, lakes, parks, and other natural places will usually be italicized.

---

### EXERCISE 4

*Read the following passage and interpret Map 3. Then, answer the questions about the passage and the map.*

### Japan's Population

Japan has the tenth-largest population of all the countries on earth, but it has only the 62nd-largest land area in the world. More than 127,000,000 people live on a string of islands smaller than the state of California. In addition, most of the interior of the central island, Honshu, is covered with mountains. Therefore, millions of people live in the crowded metropolitan areas near the sea. This large population living in a small area is in sharp contrast to many of the other most populous countries such as China, the United States, Russia, India, and Brazil. These countries also have millions (or billions) of people, but they have much larger land areas for people to inhabit.

## Map 3: Japan's Population

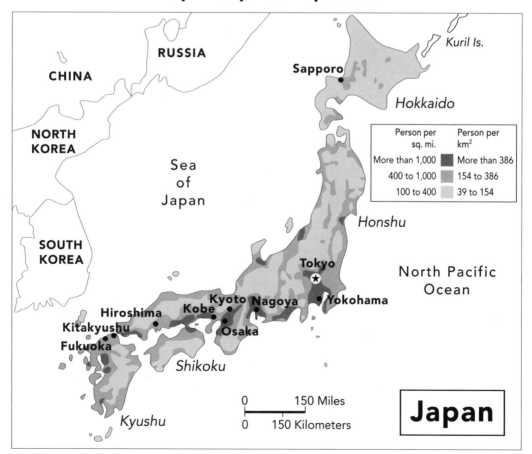

1. What subject does the passage address? _____

_____

2. What is Japan's ranking among all countries in population? _____

_____

3. What is Japan's ranking among all countries in size?

_____

4. Does the map show you where Japan is located in the world? _____

_____

5. What information does the map illustrate about Japan? _____

_____

6. Using the map and the information presented in the reading passage, describe where most people in Japan live. _(Be as specific as you can.)_

_____

_____

_____

_____

7. Why do most people live in the areas you mentioned in the previous question?

_____

_____

# Reading and Interpreting Graphs

Graphs are illustrated sources of information that usually show changes in something over a period of time. You may encounter graphs in almost every field of study.

Graphs can show information such as:

- changes in rainfall in an area
- changes in immigration in a particular country
- changes in the sale of a product
- or changes in many other things

The information in graphs can be used to show trends or to make comparisons between different periods of time. It can also help you predict what may happen in the future based on past trends.

Graphs can be created in different ways. **Bar graphs** and **line graphs** are the most common. These graphs include the same information, and you can read each graph the same way, but they look different.

## ◎ Reading a Graph

1. Read the title.

2. Look at the vertical and horizontal axes (the lines on the side and bottom of the graph).

3. Look at the patterns shown in the graph.

## ▼ Bar Graphs

### EXERCISE 1

*Look at the following bar graph and answer the questions that follow.*

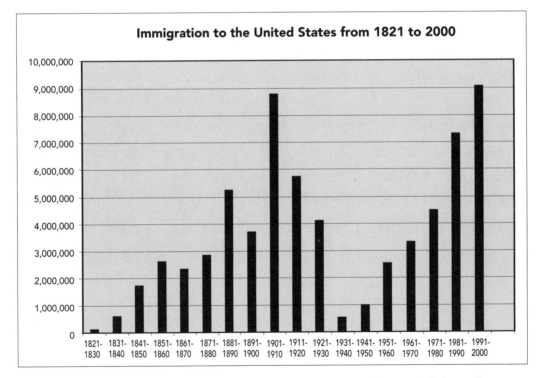

**Immigration to the United States from 1821 to 2000**

*Source:* Projections and graph courtesy of Population-Environment Balance, Sources: U.S. Census Bureau, Statistical Yearbook, Bureau of Citizenship and Immigration Services

1. Look at the title. What information does this graph provide?

   _____

2. Look at the vertical (up-and-down) axis. What do these numbers mean?

   _____

3. Look at the horizontal axis on the bottom of the graph. What are these numbers?

   _____

4. Which pattern does the graph show?

   a. United States immigration has always been constant.

   b. There have been several waves of immigration.

   c. Immigration has increased every year in American history.

5. From the pattern you see in the graph, what will probably happen in the future?

   a. Immigration will increase every year.

   b. Immigration will decrease every year.

   c. There will be a decrease in immigration followed by an increase.

**EXERCISE 2**

*Next, look at the following bar graph.*

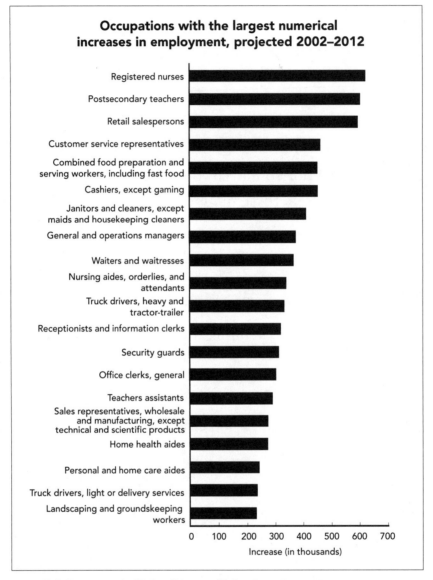

**Occupations with the largest numerical increases in employment, projected 2002–2012**

*Source:* U.S. Department of Labor, Bureau of Labor Statistics

1. What about this graph is different from the bar graph on page 60?

_____

_____

2. Look at the title. Rephrase the title to explain to someone what information is presented in the graph.

_____

_____

3. What information is presented on the vertical axis?

_____

_____

4. What information is presented on the horizontal axis?

_____

_____

5. If you were trying to choose a job that would be in demand when you graduate, which would you choose?

_____

6. Which fields show increases in employment?

    a. health care

    b. sales

    c. food service

    d. all of the above

7. Which field does not show much increase in employment?

    a. education

    b. cashiers

    c. truck driving (light or delivery services)

## ▼ Line Graphs

### EXERCISE 3

*Now, look at the following line graph. Remember that although it may look a little different from the bar graphs you have seen, you can read the information in the same way. You are researching information on automobile accidents in the town of Springfield. Use this line graph to answer the following questions.*

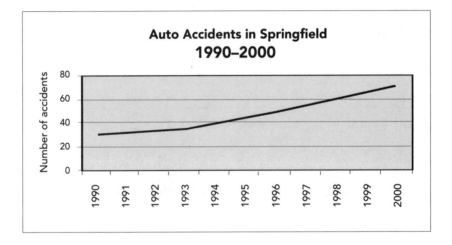

1. What trends do you notice in the number of automobile accidents from 1990–2000 in Springfield? Explain your answer with the information presented in the graph.

_____

_____

_____

2. What can you predict would happen to automobile accidents in this town if nothing changes?

_____

_____

_____

3. What would you suggest that the town do to reduce the number of automobile accidents in the future?

_____

_____

_____

## EXERCISE 4

_Look at the following line graph, and answer the questions that follow._

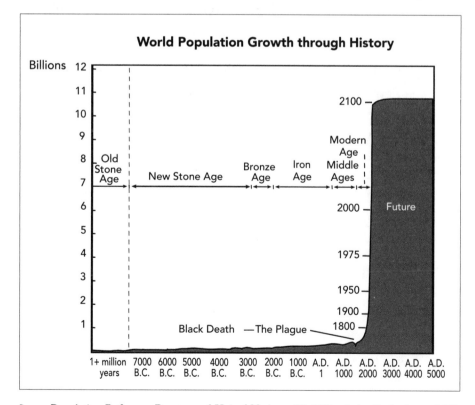

_Source:_ Population Reference Bureau; and United Nations, _World Population Projections to 2100_ (1998)

1. What does this graph show?

_____

2. What do the numbers on the vertical axis represent?

_____

3. What do the numbers on the horizontal axis represent?

_____

4. What trend do you see?

_____

5. What do you think this information means?

_____

6. What kind of problems do you think the world might face if world population continues to grow at the current rate?

_____

_____

_____

# Reading and Interpreting Charts and Tables

## ▼ Pie Charts

There are other types of illustrated information you may encounter in your studies. A **pie chart** looks like a pie and illustrates how information is divided by number or percentage.

Pie charts can show information such as:

- how many people support different political candidates
- reasons why people do something
- how many people agree, disagree, or have no opinion on an issue
- numbers or percentages related to other information

### ◎ Reading a Pie Chart

✓ Read the title.

✓ Read the legend (the key that explains what each piece of the pie represents).

✓ Look at the sizes of each piece of the pie (numbers and percentages may or may not be written on the chart).

The information shown in pie charts can help you see the differences between the parts of a whole. Like graphs, pie charts can be used to determine trends or to make predictions.

## EXERCISE 1

*Look at the following pie chart. It shows how people in one county in the United States voted in one election.*

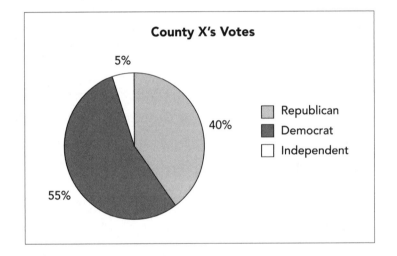

1. For which political party did the most people in County X vote?

   _____

2. For which political party did the fewest people in County X vote?

   _____

3. What does this chart tell you about the voting habits in County X?

> a. Most people in the county voted.
>
> b. More people supported the Democratic Party than the Republican Party.
>
> c. More people in the county supported the Republican Party than the Democratic Party.

## EXERCISE 2

*Look at the following pie chart. A company is considering opening a coffee shop in a certain area. The company surveyed 50 people who live in the area to see if they would be potential customers.*

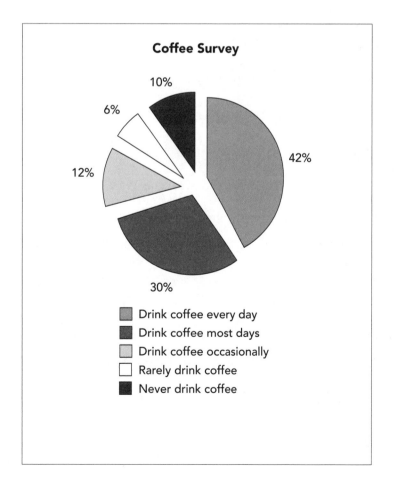

**Coffee Survey**

10%
6%
42%
12%
30%

- Drink coffee every day
- Drink coffee most days
- Drink coffee occasionally
- Rarely drink coffee
- Never drink coffee

Suppose you were using this information for an economics class report. Based on the results of the survey, do you think the company should open a coffee shop in this area? Circle your answer.

Yes
No
Not enough information

When you look at illustrated information, you should also consider information that is not given. If you circled "Not enough information," you would be correct. Although the survey shows that most people who took it said they drink coffee regularly, there is other information missing that should be considered before a decision to open a coffee shop is made.

### EXERCISE 3

*What information **doesn't** the chart show that should be considered before opening a coffee shop? Circle all that apply.*

    a.  How many people surveyed like coffee

    b.  How many people live in the area

    c.  How many other coffee shops are in the area

    d.  Whether the people surveyed would prefer to buy their coffee at coffee shops or whether they would prefer to make their own

    e.  Whether people in the area feel that they need a new coffee shop

    f.  Whether people like regular or decaffeinated coffee

    g.  Whether people drink coffee for breakfast only or at other times during the day

## ▼ Tables

Tables provide much of the same kind of information that may be found in charts or graphs. Tables are often used when there is a great deal of information that would not be easy to read in a graph or chart. The information may or may not show any trends or patterns. Tables can be organized by year, by number (largest to smallest), by alphabetical order, or by other patterns.

### ◎ Reading Tables

1. Read the title.
2. Look at the rows and columns. Determine what information is provided.
3. Determine how the table is organized.

### EXERCISE 4

*Suppose you are writing a research paper on weather. You want to see if temperatures are increasing. Look at the table on page 72 of the average temperatures in Chicago in January. Answer the questions that follow the table.*

## Average January Temperature
## Chicago, IL

| Year | Temperature |
|------|-------------|
| 2004 | 21.0 °F |
| 2003 | 21.3 °F |
| 2002 | 31.9 °F |
| 2001 | 24.5 °F |
| 2000 | 25.3 °F |
| 1999 | 22.6 °F |
| 1998 | 29.5 °F |
| 1997 | 18.7 °F |
| 1996 | 23.3 °F |
| 1995 | 24.0 °F |
| 1994 | (no data) |
| 1993 | 26.2 °F |
| 1992 | 29.6 °F |
| 1991 | 20.7 °F |
| 1990 | 33.9 °F |
| 1989 | 32.4 °F |
| 1988 | 19.7 °F |
| 1987 | 25.9 °F |
| 1986 | 22.8 °F |
| 1985 | 14.4 °F |
| 1984 | 17.1 °F |
| 1983 | 26.3 °F |
| 1982 | 12.1 °F |
| 1981 | 22.6 °F |
| 1980 | 23.4 °F |

*Source:* U.S. National Weather Service

1. Do you notice any trend or pattern in the temperatures?

_____

2. Does it appear that the temperatures are increasing every year?

_____

3. If you were writing a paper on global warming, would this table support the view that the world is getting warmer? Why or why not?

_____

_____

_____

## EXERCISE 5

_Now, you are researching the British election of 1997 to determine how the British government changed during the 1990s. You find the following table of information that shows how many seats in Parliament each political party won in the election. Read the following questions and find the answers in the table._

1. Which political party or parties won the most seats?

_____

2. Which political party or parties won the fewest seats?

_____

3. How is this table structured? (Why is the Labour Party listed first?)

_____

_____

4. Even if you have no prior knowledge of British politics, which political party seems to have had the most influence in the British Parliament following the 1997 elections? Why?

_____

_____

5. For your research paper, what could you determine was the biggest change in the British Parliament during the 1997 elections based on the information presented in the table?

_____

_____

_____

| Party | Seats | Gains/Losses | % Vote |
|---|---|---|---|
| Labour (Tony Blair) | 419 | +146 | 44.4% |
| Conservative (William Hague) | 165 | -178 | 31.4% |
| Liberal Democrats (Paddy Ashdown) | 46 | +29 | 17.2% |
| Scottish National Party (SNP) (Alex Salmond) | 6 | | 2.0% |
| Plaid Cymru (Welsh Nationalists) | 4 | | 0.5% |
| Ulster Unionist Party (UUP) (David Trimble) | 10 | | |
| SDLP (John Hume) | 3 | | |
| Sinn Fein (Gerry Adams) | 2 | | |
| Democratic Unionists (Ian Paisley) | 2 | | |
| UK Unionists | 1 | | |
| Independent | 1 | | |

*Source:* British Studies Information and Resources

# Review—Practicing Skills from Part 2

## ▼ Practicing What You Have Learned

In this part, you learned how to read and interpret illustrated information such as maps, graphs, and charts. Usually, illustrated information will accompany readings, but you can get information quickly and decide if the reading is helpful to you by looking at the illustrated information.

### EXERCISE 1: TABLES

*Suppose you are doing research on earthquakes for a science class. Use the following illustrated information to help you decide what specific earthquake topic would be best for your research.*

| Number of Earthquakes in the United States for 2000–2003 | | | | |
|---|---|---|---|---|
| Magnitude | 2000 | 2001 | 2002 | 2003 |
| 8.0 to 9.9 | 0 | 0 | 0 | 0 |
| 7.0 to 7.9 | 0 | 1 | 1 | 2 |
| 6.0 to 6.9 | 10 | 5 | 5 | 7 |
| 5.0 to 5.9 | 60 | 45 | 70 | 61 |
| 4.0 to 4.9 | 287 | 294 | 538 | 465 |
| 3.0 to 3.9 | 913 | 834 | 1525 | 1,369 |
| 2.0 to 2.9 | 657 | 646 | 1,228 | 704 |
| 1.0 to 1.9 | 0 | 2 | 2 | 2 |
| 0.1 to 0.9 | 0 | 0 | 0 | 0 |
| No Magnitude | 415 | 434 | 507 | 336 |
| Total | 2,342 | 2,261 | 3,876 | 2,946 |
| Estimated Deaths | 0 | 0 | 0 | 2 |

*Source:* U.S. Geological Survey

1. Describe the information illustrated in this table.

   _____

   _____

2. Does this information appear helpful for your research?

   _____

   _____

3. Does the number of earthquakes appear to have increased between 2000 and 2003?

   _____

4. Does the number of earthquake deaths appear to have increased between 2000 and 2003?

_____

5. What data from the table could you use for your research?

_____

_____

_____

## EXERCISE 2: GRAPHS

_Look at the following graph, and answer the questions that follow._

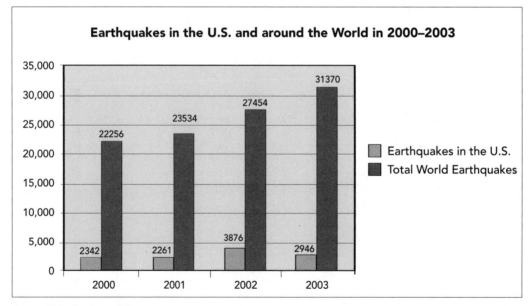

**Earthquakes in the U.S. and around the World in 2000–2003**

_Source:_ U.S. Geological Survey

1. What information is illustrated in this graph?

   _____

   _____

2. Does it appear that earthquakes increased around the world every year between 2000 and 2003?

   _____

3. Does it appear that earthquakes increased in the United States every year between 2000 and 2003?

   _____

4. Remember to think about information that is not illustrated. Suppose you read that scientists do not believe that the number of earthquakes is actually increasing. If that's true, how could you explain the data in this chart?

   _____

   _____

   _____

5. What data from the table could you use for your research?

   _____

   _____

**EXERCISE 3: MAPS**

*The surface of Earth is made up of plates. When these plates move and rub together, they cause earthquakes. Look at the following tectonic map (a map of Earth's plates), and answer the questions that follow.*

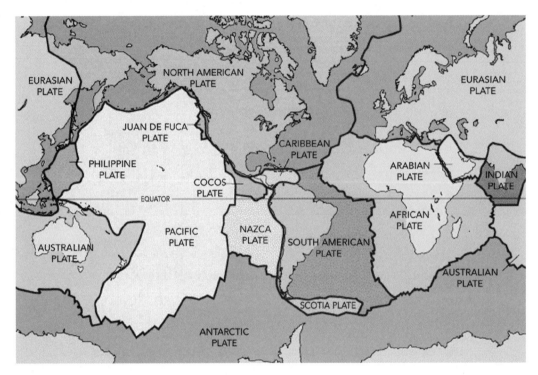

*Source:* U.S. Geological Survey

1. On what plate is the United States (except Hawaii) located?

   _____

2. What plates touch the United States' plate?

   _____

   _____

3. Near which states do these plates touch?

   _____

   _____

4. Which states would seem to have the most earth-quakes based on this information?

_____

_____

5. What information does this map give you that you could use for your research?

_____

_____

_____

## EXERCISE 4: PIE CHART

_Use the pie chart to answer the questions that follow._

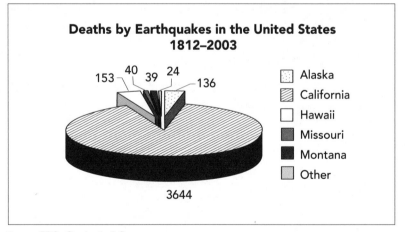

**Deaths by Earthquakes in the United States 1812–2003**

153  40  39  24  136

Alaska
California
Hawaii
Missouri
Montana
Other

3644

_Source:_ U.S. Geological Survey

1. In which U.S. state do most earthquake deaths occur?

_____

2. Look at the tectonic map and your answers to the questions that followed it. Explain why the state that has the most earthquakes does so.

_____

_____

3. What information could you use from this chart for your research?

_____

_____

## EXERCISE 5: CONSOLIDATING INFORMATION

1. Now, look at all of the illustrated information about tectonic plates and earthquakes as well as your answers to each question. With the information you have, about what specific topic could you write for your research? _(Note: You don't have to use all of the illustrated information.)_

_____

_____

_____

2. What information would you still need in order to write your research paper _(based on the topic you wrote for your answer to question 1)_?

_____

_____

# PART 3

# Skills for
# Better Reading

# Determining the Main Idea

Most of the writing you read at school (and the presentations you hear) have a **main idea**—one point the writer or speaker is trying to make clearest to you.

Main ideas may be hard to find because:

1. other ideas are all around them
2. the writer may never say directly what the main idea is

Look at the following passage.

(1)      Birds are built not just to fly but to survive heat and cold

(2)    that would kill most humans. The structural features of a

(3)    feather are a key element in helping the animal maintain

(4)    its body temperature. A strong hollow tube, the

(5)    shaft, runs the entire length of a feather. This is

(6)    made of keratin (as is a fingernail), which is light

(7)    but strong, the perfect material for trapping

(8)    pockets of air inside a hollow space.

(9)      Birds have different kinds of feathers, but

(10)  what we usually think of as a feather is a "contour feather."

(11)  These lie flat on the bird's body and overlap to give the

(12)  body its shape. The shaft of a contour feather is covered

(13)  with a layer of flat, hook-like structures called barbs (except

(14)  on the wing and tail feathers, which must remain free to

(15)  direct the bird in flight).  The barbs keep overlapping

(16)  feathers together and create even more air pockets between

(17)  them. The soft fiber-like parts of a feather make up the

(18)  vane. There is a lot of air between strands of a contour

(19)  feather's vanes, and between the various contour feathers

(20)  as they lie on the bird's body. This air, plus that inside the

(21)  shaft, forms an insulation very valuable to an animal that

(22)  spends most of its time outside.


Check the line that you think best expresses the main idea of this reading.


_____ 1. Birds

_____ 2. Feathers

_____ 3. The structure of a feather

_____ 4. The structure of a feather helps keep a bird
              from being too warm or too cold.

_____ 5. The structure of a feather helps a bird fly and
              keep warm.

The statement in Line 4 is closest to the main idea of this paragraph. There are other ideas in the paragraph:

- Feathers are strong.
- Feathers are made of the same material as fingernails.
- Birds have many types of feathers.
- Contour feathers overlap.
- The wing and tail feathers must be free.

Each of these is interesting, and the author wants us to understand them, but none of them is the main idea. Each one represents only a piece of what the writer wants to say. When you add them all up, you come up with the main idea.

---

### √ Tips: Finding the Main Idea

In a well-written piece of writing, a **main idea:**

✓ makes a statement

✓ covers all the information in a piece, like an umbrella

✓ is mentioned often, in many words whose meaning is related

✓ is probably stated somewhere near the beginning or end

## EXERCISE 1

*Answer the following questions regarding the reading about feathers.*

1. The reading says that the _____ of feathers provides _____ for a bird.

2. Find as many words as you can that refer to "insulation" or "keeping warm." If you find an item more than once, list it more than once. (One item is already on the list to get you started.)

   pockets of air

3. Find a sentence near the beginning or end of the reading that expresses the main idea.

   _____

   _____

## ▼ Topics versus Statements

A main idea always says something about a topic—it does *not* just name it. The main idea is a claim or a statement, not just a topic.

| Topic | Statement <u>about</u> the Topic |
|---|---|
| car racing | Surveys have shown that most fans of car racing are politically conservative. |
| Shakespeare's *Othello* | Several ideas about race are expressed in Shakespeare's play *Othello*. |
| the Louisiana Purchase | The Louisiana Purchase suddenly changed the course of U.S. history. |
| animals in space | Some animal-rights groups have objected to the practice of sending animals into space. |
| the harm done by presidential assassinations | Presidential assassination is destructive in many ways, but primarily because it causes presidents to be cautious and distant from the public. |

Notice that the last "topic" is like a statement, but it is very weak. It states the obvious: assassinations are harmful. The corresponding "statement" is much stronger.

## EXERCISE 2

*Mark each of the following as a topic (T) or a statement about a topic (S).*

_____ 1. The similarities between dinosaurs and modern birds

_____ 2. Rust-free metals

_____ 3. Despite certain similarities, birds probably did not share an ancestor with any known dinosaur.

_____ 4. Broken treaties about land between the federal government and the Indian tribes

_____ 5. The World Court is in The Hague (Netherlands), and the headquarters of the European Union is in Brussels (Belgium).

_____ 6. The importance of multi-national organizations

_____ 7. The amount of federal income tax that most people pay has dropped since 1960.

_____ 8. I pay taxes to the federal government.

Notice that a verb is necessary to turn a topic into a statement.

**EXERCISE 3: CRITICAL THINKING—DISCUSSION**

*Even though items 5 and 8 are full sentences with verbs, each is unlikely to be the main idea of a piece of writing. Why?*

## ▼ The Umbrella Principle

The main idea is like an umbrella that covers all of the ideas in a piece of writing. If a large part of the writing does not relate to an idea, that idea is probably not the main idea.

**EXERCISE 4**

*Read the following paragraph, which contains two sentences that don't fit under the umbrella of the main idea. Answer the following questions about the reading.*

The ridge region of western Minnesota and eastern South Dakota illustrates one glacier-caused feature—the moraine. Buffalo Ridge is made of material pushed southwestward at the edge of the sheet of ice. Today, this region is governed partly by the states of Minnesota and South Dakota and partly by the Sisseton Band of the Lakota. Many lakes of Wisconsin and Minnesota illustrate another, the "pothole." Pothole lakes (also known as kettle lakes) were formed by pieces of ice broken off the main ice sheet and left behind as it retreated northeastward. These compressed the land into holes that subsequently filled with stream water. The craters, or caldera, of volcanoes also often form lakes. Another glacial reminder in our current geology is the rich layer of farmland in many parts of the upper Midwest. Here, layers of easily tilled soil—known as drift—show how finely a river of ice can pulverize some of the rock it travels over.

1. What is the main idea of the reading?

_____

_____

_____

_____

2. Which two sentences do not fit in with this main idea?

    a. _____

    _____

    _____

    b. _____

    _____

    _____

3. If you have correctly found the main idea, you will recognize that the reading lists three landscape features as support for this main idea. List these three features:

a. _____

b. _____

c. _____

## ▼ Repetition of the Main Idea

A main idea will be mentioned often in a reading. It may not be mentioned in every sentence, but it will appear in many.

The author may not use the same words for an important idea each time. That would make the writing boring. In the reading about glacial effects on the land, notice the many different references to glaciers:

glacial

glacier

ice sheet

it

river of ice

sheet of ice

The pronoun *it* is included in this list. Pronouns contribute a lot to the variety of reference in a discussion of the main idea.

## EXERCISE 5

*Read the following passage, and answer the questions that follow it.*

Northeastern Asia is the normal home of the emerald ash borer *(Agrilus planipennis)*. In 2002, however, this insect was identified in southeast Michigan by researchers associated with Michigan State University. It is now one of the most feared exotic species among tree experts in the U.S. and Canada. Researchers fear an outbreak as destructive as the Dutch elm disease of 30 years ago.

In other tree diseases like oak wilt, which is a fungus, an insect is merely the carrier of a harmful agent. In this case, the bug itself is the problem. The ash trees it attacks die because the borer eats it, from the inside out.

It's hard to tell which ash trees are infected already, because the bug lays its eggs under the bark. Because of this, 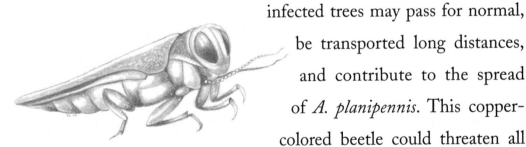 infected trees may pass for normal, be transported long distances, and contribute to the spread of *A. planipennis*. This copper-colored beetle could threaten all 16 species of ash tree in the Eastern U.S. Once infected, a tree has only about 3 years to live. In its last days, the tree looks truly sick, with almost no foliage and holes showing where the borer has chewed its way out of the tree on reaching adulthood.

1. Which of the following is the main idea of the reading?

   a. The emerald ash borer must eat its way out of an ash tree on reaching adulthood.

   b. The emerald ash borer presents a new threat to North America's trees.

   c. As demonstrated by the emerald ash borer's arrival from Asia, harmful insects can travel from one country to another.

   d. In most tree diseases, unlike the ash borer infestation, an insect simply carries a disease.

2. List at least six other terms from this passage that refer to the emerald ash borer.

   _____      _____

   _____      _____

   _____      _____

## EXERCISE 6: CRITICAL THINKING

1. What do you think was the author's purpose in writing this article about the ash borer?

   _____

   _____

   _____

   _____

2. Why does the author mention other diseases in such a short piece of writing?

   _____

   _____

   _____

   _____

# ▼ A Direct Statement

Sometimes, the main idea is directly stated in an essay or a paragraph. A direct statement of the main idea for a whole essay is called a **thesis statement**. A direct statement of the main idea of a single paragraph is called a **topic sentence**.

Unfortunately, you cannot be sure that such a sentence exists. If it does, here are some places you might find it.

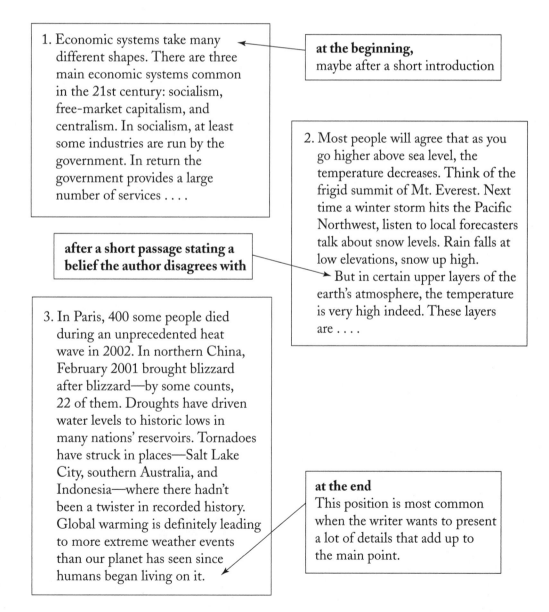

1. Economic systems take many different shapes. There are three main economic systems common in the 21st century: socialism, free-market capitalism, and centralism. In socialism, at least some industries are run by the government. In return the government provides a large number of services . . . .

**at the beginning,**
maybe after a short introduction

2. Most people will agree that as you go higher above sea level, the temperature decreases. Think of the frigid summit of Mt. Everest. Next time a winter storm hits the Pacific Northwest, listen to local forecasters talk about snow levels. Rain falls at low elevations, snow up high. But in certain upper layers of the earth's atmosphere, the temperature is very high indeed. These layers are . . . .

**after a short passage stating a belief the author disagrees with**

3. In Paris, 400 some people died during an unprecedented heat wave in 2002. In northern China, February 2001 brought blizzard after blizzard—by some counts, 22 of them. Droughts have driven water levels to historic lows in many nations' reservoirs. Tornadoes have struck in places—Salt Lake City, southern Australia, and Indonesia—where there hadn't been a twister in recorded history. Global warming is definitely leading to more extreme weather events than our planet has seen since humans began living on it.

**at the end**
This position is most common when the writer wants to present a lot of details that add up to the main point.

## EXERCISE 7

*What is the main idea in each passage (1–3)?*

1. _____

   _____

   _____


2. _____

   _____

   _____


3. _____

   _____

   _____

# Types of Writing on Assignments and Tests

You can't answer a test question correctly if you don't know what it is asking for. Teachers have certain expectations for the kind of writing you will produce in response to their questions and assignments. This lesson will help you understand some of these expectations.

## ▼ Appropriate Levels of Formality

You write differently for different purposes. For an e-mail or a note to a friend, you use different words, patterns of organization, and even grammar than you would use in a report for your teacher.

Things that are too **informal** are not **appropriate** (not in the right style) for a class paper. Similarly, things that are too formal in a **letter** to a friend are inappropriate because they will seem cold or rude.

## EXERCISE 1

_Mark each of the following words or expressions as appropriate **(A)** or not appropriate **(N)** for the given writing situation._

_____ 1. A term paper for a class: "There are many reasons why Earth's tropical zone is being deforested."

_____ 2. A note to a friend: "Kindly phone me at your earliest convenience."

_____ 3. An e-mail to a friend: "Don't want to have lunch with me, huh? Where were you?"

_____ 4. An answer on a test: "Surveys show that most liposuction is done on rich people. They just want to look better than everybody else. Well, whatever. It's their money."

_____ 5. A note to one of your teachers: "Sorry I missed your class, man. Nothing personal. I just partied too hard last night."

_____ 6. An answer on a quiz: "My in-depth analysis of the world view that allowed slavery leads me to pause and consider the conditions in which we find ourselves now. Oh, how horrible it is when one man enchains another!"

_____ 7. An entry in a journal for your literature class: "Spent the whole weekend trying to like Henry James. It's way too stiff! I have to shake myself awake sometimes."

_____ 8. A term paper for a class: "Asymmetric application of theorems yields asymmetric conclusions regardless of the validity of the theorem under consideration."

_____ 9. A note to your parents: "I'm gone. I'll be back some time, I guess. I don't know."

_____10. An answer on a test: "Although there is some controversy over who invented the laser, this achievement is usually credited to Arthur Schawlow and Charles Townes."

## EXERCISE 2: DISCUSSION

*Compare your answers with those of another student or with your whole class. Why did you answer as you did? In particular, discuss your answers to items 6, 7, and 8.*

### √ Tip: Writing Formally

For most assignments and on most tests, your teacher is probably expecting a moderate level of formality—not too fancy and not too familiar. Your teacher might make an exception for highly personal kinds of writing, like a journal.

## ▼ Genres

A **genre** is a kind of writing. There are many different genres, including:

- detective stories
- news articles
- editorials
- self-help books
- romantic novels
- personal letters
- classroom papers
- short answers on quizzes
- friendly e-mails
- business e-mails

### EXERCISE 3

*Name at least three more genres of writing.*

_____

_____

_____

A writer working in a certain genre is expected to write in a certain way. Once readers recognize a certain genre, they expect certain things. For example, someone writing a detective story is expected to write about a puzzling crime that the main character will solve. Readers will be disappointed if there is no crime or if it is too easy to solve.

Someone writing a sales letter is expected to tell why a product or service is good and explain how the receiver of the letter can buy it. If this information is not included, the potential customer will be confused.

These expected structures—along with certain vocabulary and style—make it possible to identify a genre of writing even if you don't know where the writing comes from.

## EXERCISE 4

*Label each of the following samples as belonging to one of the following genres. Be prepared to say, in a class discussion, why you answered the way you did.*

*Note:* There are ten items on this list but only six reading samples. Not every genre in this list will be used.

- a romance novel
- an answer to a comparison-contrast question on a test
- an answer to a definition question on a test
- a police report
- a horror story
- a news report about a robbery
- a persuasive essay
- a sales brochure
- an owner's manual for a product
- an entry in a personal journal

1. _____

> Turn lever "C" until it is parallel to lever "D." Using the Allen wrench provided in the kit, join upright "C" with bar "A."
>
> *Note:* Bolts will tighten without application of washers or nuts, which are built into the structure.
>
> Now turn the joined pieces 45 degrees left so that upright C is lying on the ground. Insert one 12-inch tie rod by bending the rod slightly and inserting one end in hole A, then the other end in hole B.

2. _____

What were the Committees of Correspondence?

The Committees of Correspondence were groups of leaders in Revolutionary America. Most of them were also members of the Sons of Liberty, founded by Samuel Adams. The committees made sure that revolutionary forces in one part of the colonies were aware of events in another.

3. _____

The light of the moon shone on the glowing grass across which he had just walked. Come daylight, that part of the lawn would look as normal and patchy as any other. But now, with his kiss still lingering on her lips, his steps glowed like the footfalls of some magical being.

Althea turned and walked toward the house. Nothing looked the same, now that she knew Gordon's love was hers. Each front step creaked differently. The windchime on the porch tinkled at a different pitch. If she was going to marry Gordon, there was so much to do.

4. _____

I'm not sure I can do this weekend's assignment. I try to remember all the rules for working with exponents, but I forget most of them. Especially about fractions. Our book says we are supposed to be able to do things like $x^{2/3}$ times $x^{3/4}$. Like how? Do I do the numerators first, then the denominators? But the denominators are different. I don't know what to do about this.

Mr. Jorgenson, can you please, like, explain this in class and please don't take off too many points from my homework. I want to learn this, but it's too hard!

5. _____

Nordeloos (AP)—The Nordeloos Branch of VanderBank was held up yesterday afternoon by a pair of robbers wearing ski masks. No one was hurt in the incident, which occurred at about 2:30, but teller Deb Ripkema was taken to Zeeland Community Hospital after her breathing became irregular.

Bank Manager Ted Gervais said he wasn't allowed to reveal the exact loss but "it was in the six-figure range," he said.

Police in Ottawa and Kent counties are searching for a blue or green Ford Fiesta with Illinois license plates. Witnesses say two men fled the bank parking lot in a car bearing that description.

6. _____

> As Helena ascended the stairs, she felt a cold blast of air trying to drive her down. The door. The draft, growing stronger now, was trying to keep her from the door, which began to glow an eerie green. The glow was slight at first. Then, as it strengthened, a figure began to appear on the central panel, a figure like a human face. Fighting the fiendish draft, Helena strained to get a better look. It was a human face, though deformed as if by decades of burial rot. She could barely believe her eyes. It was the face, much putrefied, of William Strong—dead since 1883—her great-great grandfather.

## ▽ GENRE AND TEST QUESTIONS

One main reason to learn about (and recognize) genre is that your class assignments and test questions each ask you to write in a certain way—in a certain genre.

Some questions will ask you to:

- narrate (tell a story)
- point out differences and similarities (comparison/ contrast)
- tell exactly what something is (definition)
- argue one point of view or another (persuasion)
- explain a personal viewpoint (expression of opinion)
- sort things or ideas into groups (classification)
- tell how a historical event occurred (chronology)
- describe the parts of something and show how they work together (analysis)

- show how a certain idea applies to everyday life
  (application)
- show why something is important (evaluation)

Some questions may ask you to use several of these genres. For example, the question, "What caused the Irish potato famine of the 1840s, and what does this episode teach us about modern farming practices?" asks for both cause/effect and application writing.

Here are some other examples of test questions that ask for answers in a certain genre—or combining certain genres.

- Describe the effects of Franklin Roosevelt's New Deal
  on the U.S. economy. (cause/effect)
- What is a quark, and why is it important in modern
  physics? (definition and evaluation)
- What is the best way to provide adequate health care
  to all Americans? (expression of personal opinion,
  analysis)

## EXERCISE 5

*After each assignment/test question below, determine which kind of writing the question is asking for.*

| | |
|---|---|
| narration | classification |
| comparison/contrast | chronology |
| definition | analysis |
| persuasion | application |
| expression of opinion | evaluation |

1. Relate Aquinas's ideas about a justifiable war to one of
   the following conflicts:

   World War II              Gulf War I (the battle
   Vietnam                       for Kuwait)
   Bosnia-Hercegovina        The invasion of Iraq

   ————————————————————————————————————

2. In your personal experience, is it really better to give
   than to receive?

   ————————————————————————————————————

3. Of course, not every small creature is an insect. Put
   the following into groups, name the group, and tell
   what special characteristic distinguishes this group
   from insects.

   shrew          spider         scorpion
   centipede      bacterium      mouse
   snake          hummingbird    shrimp
   jellyfish

   ————————————————————————————————————

4. Trace the development of pan-Arabism in Syria,
   Libya, Egypt, and Iraq during the 20th century.

   ————————————————————————————————————

5. Why should or should not the United States stay in the North American Free Trade Agreement?

   _____

6. What agencies make up the U.S. federal Security Services? Explain how they are different from one another.

   _____

7. Define *family*. Who makes it up? What determines who makes up a family?

   _____

8. Tell the story of the worst day in your life. Use explicit details to explain why it was so bad.

   _____

9. Astronomers have seen a round ball of ice and rock that orbits around our sun but is farther than Pluto. It is about 1,400 km in diameter—about the size of Pluto. Astronomers expect to find many objects of similar shape, size, and make-up in the area of this new discovery. Should this new discovery be considered a planet or not? Explain your answer.

   _____

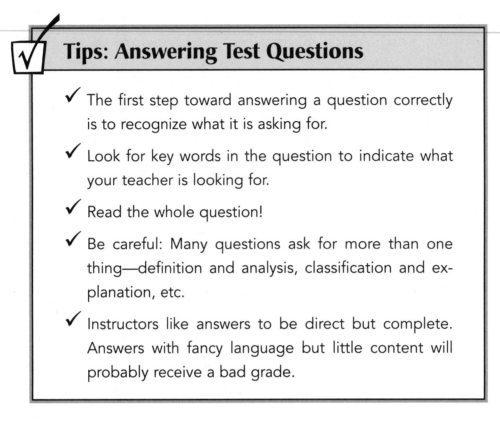

## ✓ Tips: Answering Test Questions

✓ The first step toward answering a question correctly is to recognize what it is asking for.

✓ Look for key words in the question to indicate what your teacher is looking for.

✓ Read the whole question!

✓ Be careful: Many questions ask for more than one thing—definition and analysis, classification and explanation, etc.

✓ Instructors like answers to be direct but complete. Answers with fancy language but little content will probably receive a bad grade.

# Scanning and Skimming

In both scanning and skimming, you look quickly at a piece of writing. In fact you look so quickly, you don't actually read it.

When you **scan,** you glance at a piece of writing to see what is in it—what parts it has, where certain features are, the level of difficulty, etc. When you **skim,** you look a little more specifically—for a certain word, phrase, fact, etc. But after you have found what you're skimming for, you stop. You don't actually read the piece of writing. Other types of quick reading, such as getting the basic idea of a reading, are part scanning and part skimming.

## ▼ Scanning

The following exercise asks you to scan <u>this</u> book, with which you have been working for a while. Normally, you would do this kind of scanning much earlier. Since scanning is a matter of becoming familiar with something, people usually scan a book or other reading very soon after first seeing it.

**EXERCISE 1**

*Scan this book and answer the questions. Try to work quickly. You may want to time yourself to see how fast you can answer.*

1. How many lessons (or chapters) does this book have?

   _____

2. On what page does the table of contents start? _____

3. On which pages would you find a lesson about reading maps? _____

4. On which page would you find a lesson about plagiarism? _____

5. What comes after the last lesson of this book?

   _____

## ▽ SCANNING ON THE INTERNET

The first time you go to an Internet site, you may not know what to expect. You may scan the home page to see if it's a site you want to look at more carefully.

## EXERCISE 2

*The following is adapted from the home page at* www.state.gov, *the website for the U.S. State Department. Scan the page, and answer the questions that follow.*

Home | Contact Us | Email this Page | FOIA | Privacy Notice | Archive | Español    Search [    ] GO

# U.S. DEPARTMENT *of* STATE

| About the State Dept. | Press and Public Affairs | Travel and Living Abroad | Countries and Regions | International Issues | History, Education and Culture | Business Center | Other Services | Employment |

**About the State Department**
A-Z index
Secretary of State Colin L. Powell
Senior State Department Officials
more...

**Press and Public Affairs**
Audio and Video Releases
Press Releases (Secretary)
Press Releases (Other)
more...

**Travel and Living Abroad**
Travel Warnings
Emergencies Abroad
Passports for U.S. Citizens
Visas for Foreign Citizens
more...

**Countries and Regions**
Afghanistan
Country Background Notes
U.S. Embassies, Consulates, Missions
more...

**International Topics and Issues**
Environment and Conservation
Human Rights
more...

**History, Education and Culture**
Educational and Cultural Affairs
Diplomatic History
Student Page
more...

**Business Center**
Doing Business in International Markets
Contracting Opportunities
more...

**Other Services**
Children's Services
more...

**Employment**
Civil Service
Foreign Service
Student Programs
International Organizations
more...

### HIGHLIGHTS

**U.S AMBASSADOR TO IRAQ**
**Ambassador John D. Negroponte (June 23):** "As I prepare to go to Iraq as United States Ambassador, I do so with a clear mission: to offer support and assistance to the Iraqi people and government as Iraq reasserts its full sovereignty."

**Murder of Korean Hostage Kim Sun-il in Iraq**
**Secretary Powell (June 22):** "He was an innocent man there to help the people of Iraq, cut down by senseless barbarism."

**Revisions to Patterns of Global Terrorism Released**
A review of the 2003 edition of "Patterns of Global Terrorism" determined that the data in the report was incomplete and in some cases incorrect. The corrected Year in Review, Appendix A, and Appendix G are now available.

**South Asia Assistant Secretary Rocca (June 22:)** "The next few years will provide a crucial opportunity for the United States to help South Asia become a peaceful, democratic and prosperous region, free from terror and nuclear threat." [full text]

### IN OTHER NEWS

• The United States strongly supports Iraq women's participation in the political, economic, and social reconstruction of their country.

• Deputy Assistant Secretary Bradtke testifies on U.S. initiatives at NATO's upcoming summit in Istanbul.

• The United States signs agreement to protect RMS Titanic wreck site.

• Assistant Secretary Charles testifies on Plan Colombia successes and remaining challenges.

What's NEW at state.gov      Video Connection

*Source:* U.S. Department of State, June 23, 2004, www.state.gov

1. What is found along the left edge of the webpage?

_____

_____

_____

2. What is the purpose of the buttons at the top of the page?

_____

_____

_____

3. How can you get more information about Assistant Secretary Rocca's speech?

_____

_____

_____

4. What is the purpose of the "In Other News" items at the lower right?

_____

_____

_____

## ▼ Skimming

You skim for information every day in countless places—in the newspaper, in your textbooks, and on the Internet.

### EXERCISE 3

*Add to the following list of things people commonly skim for.*

the time of a movie

a friend's address in an address book

_____

_____

_____

_____

_____

You skim for a detail—a number, a name, an amount, etc. Certain features of the text can help you. For example, a name is likely to begin with a capital letter. As you skim a longer reading, you can concentrate on looking for capital letters.

**EXERCISE 4**

*Skim the reading that follows to answer these questions.*

1. What is Georgette's last name?

2. What kind of career did Beatrice Plinth have?

3. What was the name of Georgette's husband?

4. In what town did Georgette work?

Most researchers saw cell components functionally, not etiologically. That is, they were concerned about what the parts of a cell did, not where they came from. Georgette Gold herself followed this conventional approach until reading Beatrice Plinth's 1980s research on mitochondrial DNA. Gold and a team of colleagues at Dealy College in Boston concentrated their efforts on this structure. Their comparisons of the mitochondrial DNA of 500 subjects led them to a surprising conclusion: Part of a human cell, the mitochondrio, is probably there because a clever bacterium learned how to make human cells reproduce it. When their research, authored by Gold and her husband, Thomas Fein, was published in the journal *Cellular Studies* it caused a great deal of controversy. It also led to an explosion of follow-up studies in Michigan, California, and elsewhere.

Besides names, other items can also be spotted easily because of the way they are printed. These include:

- years (always printed in numerals)
  - 1834
  - 2004
  - the mid-1970s

- times
  - in numerals with a colon—for example, 1:00
  - with A.M./P.M.—for example, seven P.M.
  - or with the word *o'clock*, which is easy to spot because it contains an apostrophe—for example, *seven o'clock*

- exact numbers higher than 12 (usually printed in numerals)
  - 135
  - 17
  - 6,467

- names of books, movies, magazines, etc. (usually italicized)
  - *The River*
  - *All's Well that Ends Well*
  - *Time* magazine

- abbreviations (usually in capital letters)
  - U.N. (for United Nations)
  - CIA (for Central Intelligence Agency)

- names of schools (usually in capital letters and containing a word like *school* or *university*)
  - Harvard University
  - James Madison High School

## EXERCISE 5

*Again, skim the reading about cell research and answer these questions.*

1. How many subjects were in the mitochondria-comparison studies done by Georgette Gold?

2. When did Beatrice Plinth do her studies on mitochondrial DNA?

3. At what university did Georgette Gold work?

4. In what journal was Gold's work published?

5. In what city was Gold working?

## ▽ SKIMMING ON THE INTERNET

Skimming is an essential skill for doing an Internet search. When you use a search engine (one of the programs that allows you to look up webpages about a certain topic), you often get a long list of hits (sites containing the word or phrase you're searching for). By skimming this list, you can see which ones seem most likely to have what you want.

## EXERCISE 6

*Imagine that for a class assignment you want to draw a diagram of the layers of Earth's atmosphere. You got the following list when you used a search engine to look for "layers of the atmosphere." Skim this list, and identify the three sites most likely to give you the information you are looking for.*

- **Bubble inside Bubble**

  Our atmosphere is threatened . . . . layers of government . . . . federal environmental regulations are inadequate to stop . . . *www.saveairforus.org/bureaucracy/html* June 2005

- **Science Survivors: A High School Survival Guide**

  Our atmosphere is usually divided into 5 layers . . . Earth's atmosphere like eggs inside each other . . . *www.sciencesurvivors.com/atmosphere/layers/html* . . . . 2005–6

- **Meteorology 101/Exercise Sheets/Montfortune University**

  Weather occurs in the troposphere . . . layer of Earth's atmosphere, . . . active atmospheric layer. *www.ymnou.edu/bograssii/101* Fall 2004

- **Atmospheric Structure: A Basic Guide to Inner Space**

  Earth's atmosphere . . . in 5 layers, to which the ionosphere is often added. Illustration shows layers of the atmosphere. Not exactly spherical. *www.themostyoucan.com* January 2004

- **Layers of the Atmosphere: Rock Lyrics: Bands: Railroad Ties**

  To move like great tectonic plates . . . love the Earth and soil . . . You add layers to my atmosphere. John Bandoliero Music. *www.songssos.com* 2004

- **National Atmospheric Administration Report on the State of the Air**

  Description of the 5 major layers of the Earth's atmosphere . . . chemical analysis at various levels in layers of the atmosphere . . . political action recommended. *www.nationalnaa.gov* undated

- **What's Up? A Fifth-Grader's Guide to What's in the Sky**
  Patterns of stars visible through the atmosphere . . .
  Atmosphere is layered like an onion. . . .
  Characteristics of each layer . . .
  *www.misterkowalski.edu/grade5/science*

- **Science Encyclopedia for the Amateur. A Basic Look.**
  Two different ways of identifing layers in the
  atmosphere, by temperature or by magnetic
  properties . . . Five layers according to temperature
  . . . Magnetic characteristics occur in layers . . .
  Make your own observations about temperature by
  climbing to the roof of the highest . . .
  *www.amateurknowledge.com/atmosphere*

## EXERCISE 7: DISCUSSION

*Compare your choices with a partner's. What differences do you see?*

*Why did you choose the ones you chose?*

Choice 1:_____

_____

Choice 2:_____

_____

Choice 3:_____

_____

**EXERCISE 8**

*Again skim through the list of Internet search hits. Answer the following questions, and fill out the "clue" blank with the part of the text that made you choose that answer. Work quickly and time yourself.*

1. Which of the sites is probably run by the government?

   Clue: _____

2. Which of the sites is probably from a university course?

   Clue: _____

3. Which of the sites is probably run by an environmentalist organization?

   Clue: _____

## ▼ Key Words

You may need to skim for facts that are not easy to see because of capital letters, numerals, etc. In that case, you may need to use the **keyword method**—find an unusual word in the question or assignment and skim for that word. The more unusual the key word the better. Very common words will not help you zero in on the part you want.

## EXERCISE 9: DISCUSSION

*Imagine that you have some readings containing the answers to the following questions. (The readings themselves are not printed here; you don't need to see them in order to do this exercise.) Which key words from the question would you skim for in order to answer correctly?*

1. What was the role of rats in the spread of diseases like the bubonic plague?

2. The Union Pacific and the Central Pacific railroads, each built from a different starting point, met at Promontory, Utah. How did they mark the joining of their tracks?

3. According to Freud, what were the three parts of the human psyche?

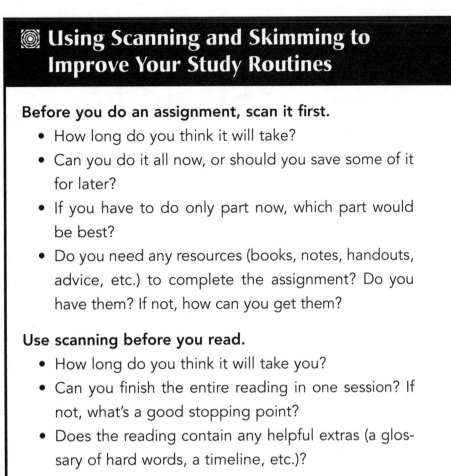

## ◉ Using Scanning and Skimming to Improve Your Study Routines

**Before you do an assignment, scan it first.**

- How long do you think it will take?
- Can you do it all now, or should you save some of it for later?
- If you have to do only part now, which part would be best?
- Do you need any resources (books, notes, handouts, advice, etc.) to complete the assignment? Do you have them? If not, how can you get them?

**Use scanning before you read.**

- How long do you think it will take you?
- Can you finish the entire reading in one session? If not, what's a good stopping point?
- Does the reading contain any helpful extras (a glossary of hard words, a timeline, etc.)?

**Use skimming to work faster on assignments and tests.**

- Does the question ask for a discrete fact?
- If so, what key words or other features can help you skim for it?
- Skim through a whole assignment or test; look for questions about the same topic. Can the answer to one question help you figure out the answer to another?

# Vocabulary Strategies

Understanding a reading involves many factors—more than a simple understanding of individual words or phrases. Still, unless you <u>do</u> understand enough of those individual words and phrases, you won't get far enough to apply your other reading skills. This lesson will give you some vocabulary strategies—general techniques for building your vocabulary and dealing with new items in a reading.

## ▼ Many Meanings

Even words you have seen—and perhaps know very well—can be a problem as you read. They may have different meanings in different contexts, and you will have to decide which meaning to apply. Think about all the meanings you know for the following words:

bear _____     freely_____

_____     _____

bright _____     hang _____

_____     _____

cast _____     map _____

_____     _____

cool _____     watch _____

_____     _____

If you have a good dictionary, it will show many meanings for the most common nouns, verbs, adverbs, and adjectives in English.

For example, depending on the context, any of the following meanings could be correct:

- **fixed** *adj.*—repaired; stable, in one position; arranged; unfairly favoring one competitor
- **definition** *nc.*—meaning of a word; clear outlines of a shape
- **remake** *vt.*—to build again, in a different way; to reform; *nc.* a new version of an old movie, television show, etc.; any newly constructed version of an old thing

> **Note:** Each dictionary has its own way of showing whether a meaning is a noun, verb, etc.
> In this book:
> *nc* = countable noun
> *nu* = uncountable noun
> *vt* = transitive verb
> *vi* = intransitive verb
> *adj* = adjective
> *adv* = adverb

Which meaning is the right one? The grammar and the context of the reading will help you decide. For example, if a reading said,

> This remake has none of the humor of the 1959 version starring Cary Grant.

your meaning clues would be:

1. One of the <u>noun</u> definitions of *remake* is right for this context, because *remake* is part of a noun phrase in this sentence.

2. The right meaning is probably "a new version of an old movie," as the context indicates.

**EXERCISE 1**

*The following are dictionary-style definitions for familiar words that have many meanings. Use these definitions to mark (with the number of the meaning from the dictionary definition) the proper meaning for the underlined word in each context. The first one is done for you as an example.*

**product**—*nc* 1. the result of a process. 2. a commodity offered for sale by a manufacturer. 3. the result of a mating or of an environment. *Steve Venables was the product of a home in which ambition and analysis were both respected.* 4. (in mathematics) the result of multiplication. *The product of 3 times 4 is 12.*

**paint**—*nu* 1. a colored liquid that can be spread on a wall or some other surface to change its color. 2. the dried form of that liquid. 3. (in basketball) a rectangular area just in front of the basket. *nc* 1. a set of containers (such as tubes) that an artist uses in painting. 2. a horse with patches of fur of different colors (see **pinto**). *vt* 1. to change something's color by applying colored liquid. 2. (usually followed by *as* or *in a ADJ light*) to portray an event or object in a certain way, usually at odds with what most people think. *The government tried to paint the invasion as an act of self-defense. vi* to have a career as an artist working with paints.

**study**—*nu* a lengthy process of finding knowledge. *nc* 1. one's academic career. 2. a process of systematic investigation or experimentation. 3. the published results of such experimentation or research. 4. a student (usually in the phrase, *a quick study*). 5. a room in which one studies; an office. *vt* 1. to look at or read about for a long time in order to gain knowledge. 2. to pursue an academic course in something. *vi* to be a student at. *I study at Cambridge.*

**shelf**—*nc,* pl. *shelves* 1. a long, flat platform, usually part of piece of furniture, on which things can be stored. 2. a projection of land under water that is shallower than the water nearby. 3. a relatively permanent and unmoving expanse of ice covering a body of water. 4. any flat, relatively thin surface with open space beneath it.

___nc 3___ 1. I read VanWieren's <u>study</u> of accidents among teenage drivers.

_____ 2. The <u>product</u> of two even numbers is always even, and the <u>product</u> of two odd numbers is always odd. What about the <u>product</u> of an even number and an odd number?

_____ 3. The president was trying to <u>paint</u> the Senate vote as support for his education policies.

_____ 4. Very little research can go on past the <u>shelf</u> unless a team is equipped with deepwater submarines.

_____ 5. Although the Astrovent van is a very safe <u>product</u>, its mechanical systems break down frequently.

_____ 6. Sitting high on his old <u>paint</u>, he looked out over the vast desert in front of him.

_____ 7. The Astrovent van is the <u>product</u> of rigorous safety testing and creative automotive design.

_____ 8. I spent my first two years of graduate school <u>studying</u> literature in Duluth.

———— 9. An analysis of a chip of <u>paint</u> from the
house showed high amounts of lead. The
entire structure would have to be stripped
and recoated before anyone could live there
again.

———— 10. Before we pass a law prohibiting the use of
this herb, more <u>study</u> is needed.

---

## ▼ Guessing the Meanings of Words from Context

---

Although context clues are not a very efficient way to learn vocabulary
in your second language, context can help you in some ways. It might
be able to help you decide among many meanings of a single word. It
can also help you guess about the meaning of vocabulary items that are
not familiar. Even if context can't tell you everything about a new vocabulary item, it might be able to give you a general idea about the
meaning.

**EXERCISE 2**

*Based on the reading, complete the exercise after it. Choose the option closest
in meaning to each underlined word or phrase. Use clues from the context to
help you decide. Be prepared to say which context clues you used in making
your decision.*

What is known as the Little Ice Age began in about
1150 and <u>lasted</u> at least 500 years. Some historians would
even claim that it didn't end until 1850. It followed the

Medieval Warm Period, which is best known for the ravages of the Vikings along the western shores of Europe.

When the climate began to turn cooler in the 12th century, Scandinavian growing seasons shortened, supplies of hay were limited, and ships encountered more sea ice. This quite simply made it hard for the Vikings to roam so freely with well-stocked ships.

The Little Ice Age also shifted the pattern of agriculture about 350 miles south. That is, a crop that might have grown in Denmark in the Medieval Warm Period now required the weather of south-central France. Substantial wine production in England or northern Germany became impossible once the full effect of the Little Ice Age was felt.

On the continent, the large-scale agriculture moved south. Whereas grain farming on the Scandinavian Peninsula is still possible, the growing season has shortened to the point where only short-season grains are practical. Grazing livestock is far more profitable than trying to bring a grain crop to maturity.

Although fish stocks throughout the North Atlantic have plummeted during the past 20 years, prior to that they were like swimming silver in the banks off Canada's coast. North European fishermen were driven to these banks by the depletion in the fish populations off Europe, thanks to the Little Ice Age. This climatic hiccup, then, was an impetus to discovery as fishermen headed toward North America and explorers such as John Cabot followed in their wake.

1. In the passage, *lasted* is closest in meaning to

    a. continued

    b. ended

    c. began

    d. measured

2. In the passage, *well-stocked* is closest in meaning to

    a. built properly

    b. carrying enough supplies

    c. armed with a lot of guns

    d. able to stand up to storms and ice

3. In the passage, *substantial* is closest in meaning to

    a. good-tasting

    b. large

    c. solid

    d. well-recorded

4. In the passage, *continent* is closest in meaning to

    a. islands

    b. conquered lands

    c. mountain

    d. mainland

5. In the passage, *maturity* is closest in meaning to

    a. good behavior

    b. old age

    c. full growth

    d. storage

6. In the passage, *plummeted* is closest in meaning to

    a. decreased slowly

    b. increased slowly

    c. decreased quickly

    d. increased quickly

7. In the passage, *banks* is closest in meaning to

    a. places to keep money

    b. riversides

    c. undersea areas

    d. places to sit

8. In the passage, *hiccup* is closest in meaning to

    a. funny thing

    b. disease

    c. short and sudden change

    d. long-term change

9. In the passage, *impetus* is closest in meaning to

     a. push

     b. barrier

     c. boat

     d. leader

10. In the passage, *in their wake* is closest in meaning to

     a. after them

     b. before them

     c. helping them

     d. keeping them alert

**EXERCISE 3: CRITICAL THINKING**

*Discuss your answers with another student or with the whole class. What evidence do you have that your answer is right? If you partner disagrees with you, what counter-evidence does he or she have? Take notes about your discussion in the space that follows.*

| My Evidence | Others' Evidence |
|---|---|
|  |  |

# ▼ Other Strategies for Learning Vocabulary

## ▽ USING WORD PARTS

Certain common word parts can be clues to the meaning of unfamiliar words. This technique does not always work, because sometimes the meaning of the word has developed far beyond the original meaning of the word part. But it is worth trying to use this if other techniques fail.

The following table lists 14 words with the most common English word parts. These parts can be recombined to make about 14,000 other English words.

## From 14 Words to 14,000 Words

| Words | Prefix | Common Meaning | Root | Common Meaning |
|---|---|---|---|---|
| 1. **precept** | *pre-* | before | *-cept* | take, seize |
| 2. **detain** | *de-* | away, down | *-ten, tain* | hold, have |
| 3. **intermittent** | *inter-* | between, among | *-mis, -mit* | send |
| 4. **offer** | *ob-* | against | *-fer* | bear, carry |
| 5. **insist** | *in-* | into | *-sist* | stand |
| 6. **monograph** | *mono-* | alone, one | *-graph* | write |
| 7. **epilogue** | *epi-* | upon | *-logue* | say, study of |
| 8. **aspect** | *ad-* | to, toward | *-spect* | see |
| 9. **uncomplicated** | *un-* com- | not together, with | *-plicate* | fold |
| 10. **nonextended** | *non-* ex- | not out, beyond | *-tend* | stretch |
| 11. **reproduction** | *re-* pro- | back, again forward, for | *-duc, -duce, -duct* | lead |
| 12. **indisposed** | *in-* dis- | not apart, not | *-pose* | put, place |
| 13. **oversufficient** | *over-* sub- | above under | *-ficient* | make, do |
| 14. **mistranscribe** | *mis-* trans- | wrong across, beyond | *-scrip, -script, -scribe* | write |

*Source:* I. S. P. Nation, *Teaching and Learning Vocabulary* (Boston: Heinle & Heinle Publishers, 1990)

## ▽ NOTEBOOKS, CARDS, OR OTHER SYSTEMS

You will learn far too many new vocabulary items to remember without some sort of system for listing them and studying them. Choose a system that works well for you. What helps one person may not help another. If a notebook works well for your friend but a card-based system works better for you, use the cards.

### A Vocabulary Notebook: Some Hints

1. Write the word to be studied close to the binding (the center) of the notebook. This will help you test yourself later.

2. Write down the word, its meaning *IN YOUR READING*, and an example of its use in *THAT* meaning. For example:

| Filter (v) | OSU scientists filtered gravel from the stream water by using ordinary window-screen mesh. | process of removing solids from a liquid by using a tool with holes |
|---|---|---|

*notice "from"*

3. As you see in this illustration, the definition should be written out at the edge of the paper. The vertical lines are places where the notepaper can be folded so you test yourself. Fold over the "meaning" part and/or the "example" part and ask yourself what a *filter* is. Also notice that you can take notes about words that commonly follow or precede your target word (for example, *from*).

4. Keep your notebook entries short.

5. If you use a dictionary to help you, focus on the meaning you need to know for your reading. <u>Do not copy down irrelevant meanings</u>.

## ▽ USING A CARD SYSTEM

Some people learn better if they write new vocabulary on notecards. They write the target word on the front of the card and meanings/examples on the back. This allows them to test themselves both ways. If they review by looking at the "meaning" side of a card, they must say what vocabulary item it goes with. If they review by looking at the vocabulary item, they try to say what the meaning or an example is.

# Review—Practicing Skills from Part 3

The four chapters before this one showed you how to **find the main idea**, decide what **type of writing** you are working with, **scan** or **skim** a reading, and **deal with the vocabulary** in the reading. Each of these activities is an element of reading strategy—a way of approaching your reading tasks efficiently and understanding what you need to.

In this review chapter, we will work with one long reading, which appears in the left column of the next few pages. In the right column, at certain points, are questions to answer about a nearby part of that reading.

## The Battle between Westinghouse and Edison

(1)    Thomas Edison and George Westinghouse were both very rich and powerful inventors by the late 1880s. These were the years in which New York City started running streetlights, streetcars, and other devices by using electrical power. It was also the time in which one of the greatest industrial competitions—the battle to electrify America—began brewing.

Scan the reading to answer the following two questions.

1. The main idea of this reading is most likely to be about
   a. inventions
   b. electrical power
   c. immigrants
   d. New York City
2. Overall, what kind of writing is this passage?
   a. chronology
   b. comparison/ contrast
   c. cause/effect
   d. persuasion

**137**

**(2)** Thomas Edison's name was already associated in the American mind with things electric. Much of the demand for electricity derived from one of his inventions, the incandescent light bulb. <u>He also had the phonograph and the movie camera to his credit.</u> It was no surprise to anyone that when New York went electric, the power was supplied by a generating plant run by the Edison General Electric Company.

**(3)** The current was a type called DC (direct current). One problem with this current was that it could not be sent more than about a mile from the place where it had been generated. To make it even that far, direct current has to be sent with a lot of force (voltage). This can melt the wires used to carry the power and can be very hazardous if a line falls.

**(4)** Another type of current, AC (alternating current) was also available as an alternative. It could be dangerous too, but it was easily transmitted over long distances and was a lot more flexible than DC. A Serbian immigrant to America, Nikola Tesla, had done a lot of work to refine the generation of AC current and was sure Thomas Edison would adopt this other form of power.

3. The underlined sentence in Paragraph 2 says that Edison
   a. liked to watch movies and listen to records
   b. bought phonographs and movie cameras
   c. produced many records and movies
   d. invented the phonograph and the movie camera

4. The main idea of Paragraph 3 is the disadvantages of
   a. electricity
   b. DC current
   c. AC current
   d. sending current long distances

5. Paragraph 4 implies that Nikola Tesla
   a. admired Edison
   b. wanted to compete with Edison
   c. disliked Edison
   d. was more flexible than Edison

**(5)** Tesla, with a letter of introduction from one of Edison's friends in Europe, went to work for Edison but soon <u>found the great man deaf to all talk of AC.</u> (In fact, Edison was hard of hearing, but that had nothing to do with his attitudes toward AC.) Edison owned patents on much of the equipment for DC generation and transfer. He did not want another form of current to devalue his patents and push DC to the sidelines.

**(6)** Disappointed, Tesla resigned from Edison's <u>employ</u> and started doing manual labor to keep food on the table. Tesla himself knew how to apply for patents, and seven of his for AC generation were granted in 1887. They did him very little good, however, if Edison had a virtual monopoly on electricity generation and if Edison was determined to stay with DC current.

**(7)** George Westinghouse enters the story at this point. He was rich and well known because he had invented an

air brake for railroad trains. He approached Tesla and offered to buy his AC patents. A partnership ensued that would eventually undo even the great Thomas Edison.

**(8)** At this point, the development of electricity could have gone either way.

6. The underlined phrase in Paragraph 5 means that
   a. Edison did not want to hear about AC
   b. Edison was very ill
   c. Edison had to have everything written down for him
   d. Edison enjoyed hearing about AC current

7. Throughout the reading, the word *patents* is used. It is closest in meaning to:
   a. the expression of an idea
   b. government recognition that you own an idea
   c. criticism of an idea
   d. permission to use someone else's idea

8. In Paragraph 6, <u>employ</u> is closest in meaning to
   a. debt
   b. use
   c. job
   d. trick

New York was using DC, but very few communities in the U.S. had any electrical system at all. They had to choose: AC or DC? Both Edison and Westinghouse attempted to influence this decision by showing how dangerous his opponent's current was. Edison arranged to have the first execution of a criminal by electric chair done with AC current. The convict suffered a horrible death—but would have done so with DC current too. What Edison didn't tell the audience was that any kind of electricity at such voltages would have produced the same result.

(9)    The death blow to DC power generation was dealt by the organizing committee for 1892's "Columbian Exposition." This world's fair, to be held in New York, was supposed to commemorate the 400th anniversary of Columbus's first voyage to the New World. It was also the first world's fair to use electric lights as a standard feature. The committee for the fair chose to use AC current generated by Westinghouse. The resulting fair was hugely successful, and AC had proven itself.

(10)    Against the protests of Edison, its founder, the General Electric Company abandoned DC platforms for AC platforms. The battle for dominance had been won by the more flexible AC.

9. The reading says that the convict's horrible death was due to
   a. electricity
   b. DC current
   c. AC current
   d. his crime

10. Where was the Columbian Exposition?
   a. Colombia
   b. Serbia
   c. New York
   d. around the world

**(11)**     Still one more battle remained for both AC and DC, and the enemy was poverty.  Battling each other cost both General Electric and Westinghouse Electric a lot of money. Building electrical power stations is an expensive process. Tesla and Westinghouse had even grander plans than most: <u>They wanted to harness the power of Niagara Falls.</u> But did they have the money to do it?

**(12)**     The financial trouble of these electric companies attracted the attention of J. P. Morgan, Cornelius Vanderbilt, and some of the other "robber barons" of the era, people who profited not by lending money to companies in distress but by buying them up and using vast amounts of cash to do what the original owners couldn't. Even a rich man like Westinghouse found it hard to finance his battle. A key turning point in Westinghouse's victory came when Tesla agreed to cancel most of his royalties (continuing income) for AC power generated by Westinghouse. Freed of this financial burden, Westinghouse attracted many new investors and built the generating stations he needed.

**(13)**     Edison had no such savior. To survive and expand, the Edison General Electric Company <u>merged</u> in 1892 with the Thomson-Houston Company to create

11. The underlined sentence in Paragraph 11 indicates that Tesla and Westinghouse
   a. wanted to use Niagara Falls to generate electricity
   b. wanted to use AC current to light up Niagara Falls
   c. wanted to use electricity to keep Niagara Falls from flowing normally
   d. wanted to move their company headquarters to Niagara Falls

12. Who solved Westinghouse's financial problems?
   a. Tesla
   b. Vanderbilt
   c. Morgan
   d. Edison

13. Which of the following is characterized as a robber baron?
   a. Thomas Edison
   b. Nikola Tesla
   c. George Westinghouse
   d. J. P. Morgan

14. In Paragraph 13, *merged* is closest in meaning to
   a. defeated
   b. helped
   c. took over
   d. joined with

the General Electric Company. Edison lost his role in the company's decision-making and was, for all practical purposes, out of the electricity-generating business. Westinghouse and Tesla had set the electricity-generating standard in the United States and the world.

**PART 4**

# Research
# Strategies

# Finding Information for Research

Libraries are good places to get information for research you may have to conduct in your studies.

What sources do libraries have that can help you find information for your research?

_____

_____

_____

## ▼ Online Catalogs

Most libraries in the United States and Canada put all of their items in an online catalog. These catalogs are convenient because you can check if they have the book, magazine, CD, or any other item you need for your research without having to go to the library. You may also be able to reserve or order a title you want through the catalog system.

┌─────────────────────────────────────────────┐
│ ✓  **Tip: Using the Online Catalog**          │
├─────────────────────────────────────────────┤
│ When looking for information in a library's online cata- │
│ log, enter as much information as you can. The more in- │
│ formation you enter, the faster you can find that │
│ information or determine if the library doesn't have it. │
│ For example, if you know the author and title of a book, │
│ you will often find information on this book faster than if │
│ you only know the author's name. │
└─────────────────────────────────────────────┘

## ▽ LIBRARY CATALOG SEARCH CATEGORIES

To find an item in the catalog, you can use several different search categories. These categories usually include key word, title, author, author/title, call number, and Library of Congress (LC) subject.

| Category | Description | Example | What to Enter in Your Search |
|---|---|---|---|
| Keywords | Important words in the subject or title | You are doing research on Charles Darwin's theory of natural selection in nature. | Darwin AND natural selection<br><br>"Operators" like AND/OR/NOT may be used between words to narrow your search. For example:<br>• *United States* AND *Civil War* brings up material on the United States during the Civil War.<br>• *Baseball* OR *basketball* will bring up material on either baseball or basketball.<br>• *York* NOT *New* will bring up material on York (in England) but not New York.<br>• *Mus** will find music, musicians, musicals, muscles, etc. |

| Category | Description | Example | What to Enter in Your Search |
|---|---|---|---|
| Title | The title of the book, CD, DVD, etc. | *The Origin of Species by Means of Natural Selection* | Origin of Species (*Note:* You usually do not need to enter words such as *the* or *a*. Sometimes, you may also shorten the title.) |
| Author | The person who wrote the book, created the music, etc. | Charles Darwin | Darwin<br><br>*or* Darwin, Charles<br><br>*or* Charles Darwin |
| Author/Title | Both the author and the title | Charles Darwin *The Origin of Species by Means of Natural Selection* | Darwin<br><br>*or* Darwin, Charles<br><br>*or* Charles Darwin Origin of Species |
| Call Number | This is the catalog number given to the item by the library. It usually consists of a number and a portion or all of the author's name. | 576.82 Darwin | 576.82 Darwin |

| Category | Description | Example | What to Enter in Your Search |
|---|---|---|---|
| (LC) Subject | *LC= Library of Congress*<br><br>The Library of Congress has a copy of every published item that has been submitted to the Library, which is put into categories based on its content. LC categories are usually very broad. | Evolution (Biology)<br><br>Natural selection | evolution<br><br>biology<br><br>natural selection |

## EXERCISE 1

*Read the following entries from a library catalog. Write in which category or categories the entry may be found. Some entries may be found in more than one category. Write all of the categories in which you think you could find this entry. Check your answers in your school or community library's online catalog.*

Example:

Shakespeare, William    <u>Author/ Keywords/LC Subject</u>

1. Ulysses _____

2. 979.3033 Martinez_____

3. Space Exploration _____

4. Carver_____

    Where I'm Calling From _____

5. fish _____

6. Abraham Lincoln _____

7. Dylan, Bob OR folk _____

8. Greece_____

9. Venice travel _____

10. J921 Trammell _____

## ▼ Online Searches

The Internet is another important way to find information for your research. You can use search engines to find websites providing information on the topic you are researching.

What are some advantages of using Internet sources instead of library sources?

What are some disadvantages of using Internet sources instead of library sources?

---

### √ Tip: Using the Internet for Research

When looking for information on the Internet, be careful about the sources you use. Some sites may only include people's opinions on a subject. Some sites may not have accurate information. Other sites may be reliable and have accurate and up-to-date facts.

### *Question:*

What kinds of websites can you usually trust to provide you with accurate factual information for your research?

## EXERCISE 2

*Using a search engine, look for a reliable website to provide you with information for research on the following topics. Write the URL (Internet address) of each website next to each topic.*

1. population growth _____

2. preventing identity theft_____

3. artificial intelligence  _____

4. the U.S. space program since 1980  _____

5. the human genome project_____

6. mad cow disease _____

7. American blues music_____

8. statistics on poverty in South Africa _____

9. effective diets for losing weight _____

10. personality disorders _____

## EXERCISE 3

*You are conducting research on various topics for various classes. Find the resources you need to complete your research using your library's online catalog or the Internet. Pick the categories that will help you find the information you need the fastest.*

| Your research assignment | Where would you search first: an online library catalog or the Internet? | Why would you search there first? | What would you enter for your search? |
| --- | --- | --- | --- |
| 1. You are writing a paper in a Sociology class on motorcycle gangs. Your teacher suggests using Hunter S. Thompson's book, *Hell's Angels*. | | | |
| 2. You are researching the work of physicist Stephen Hawking for a physics class. | | | |
| 3. You are studying the success of the McDonald's fast-food chain for an economics class. | | | |
| 4. You want to write a paper on the government of China for a political science class. | | | |
| 5. You need to research AT&T and the company's influence on long-distance telephone rates for a tele-communications class. | | | |
| 6. You need to know what year the Nobel Peace Prize began and why it is given every year. | | | |
| 7. You need to research population growth or decline in Saudi Arabia. | | | |

## EXERCISE 4

*Now, use your school or community's online card catalog or the Internet to find the information you need for the topics in Exercise 3. Check the source that you wrote you would check first. Write the title of the book or the name of the website, the author or organization that created the book or website, the date of publication or last update, and the call number or URL of the source (or of one of the sources) you find for each number. If you found the information where you expected to find it first, check the last box.*

| Title or name of website | Author | Date of publication or last update | Call number or URL | Found the information where I expected to find it first |
|---|---|---|---|---|
| 1. | | | | |
| 2. | | | | |
| 3 | | | | |
| 4. | | | | |
| 5. | | | | |
| 6. | | | | |
| 7. | | | | |

How many items did you check?

_____

Was there any information you didn't find first where
you expected to find it?

_____

_____

If information wasn't where you thought you could find
it, why do you think there wasn't any information there?

_____

_____

# Avoiding Plagiarism

Plagiarism is the act of using someone else's ideas and words without acknowledging the source. Plagiarism can be hard to avoid because you will be expected to use others' ideas and research to support your point. However, you must paraphrase others' ideas or give them proper credit.

## EXERCISE 1

*Based on the definition you just read, which of the following would be an example of plagiarism?*

1. You copied and pasted a section from an Internet article directly into your research paper.

2. You read a description of a culture in a history textbook and wrote that description with a few different words.

3. You found a quote from a famous person and included that in your paper without mentioning where you found it.

All of the previous situations are examples of plagiarism. Plagiarism is a very difficult problem to avoid. Even some famous great writers have been accused of plagiarism. However, if you remember a few simple rules, you should be able to avoid plagiarizing others.

## ◎ Avoiding Plagiarism

**Rule 1: Read someone else's words, and then write your own words. Do not copy.**

It is very easy to copy someone else's words, even if you aren't trying. Read a passage, put it away, and write your own words based on what you just read. This process is called *paraphrasing*. A paraphrase should look very different from the original but should contain most of the same main ideas.

## EXERCISE 2

*Choose the best paraphrase. Remember that the paraphrase should look very different from the original passage, but it should contain the same main ideas. To choose the best paraphrase, circle the main ideas in the original passage and in the paraphrase. The paraphrase should state the ideas in a different way.*

| Original Passage | Paraphrase |
|---|---|
| 1. There are three stages of teacher development. During the first stage, a teacher realizes that (s)he is a teacher. During the second stage, (s)he becomes comfortable with the fact that (s)he is a teacher, but realizes that (s)he needs to master the content being taught. In the third stage, a teacher is confident and knowledgeable and is now able to focus only on the needs of his/her students. | A teacher goes through three stages of development. In stage one, the teacher realizes that he or she is a teacher. In stage two, the teacher must master the content being taught. In stage three, the teacher can focus on the needs of the student. |

| Original Passage | Paraphrase |
|---|---|
| 2. In 1954, *Brown vs. Board of Education* set a legal precedent that stated that the process of sending black children and white children to different schools in parts of the United States was not fair. The black schools were usually not as good as the white schools, having less money and fewer modern texts and supplies. So, the U.S. Supreme Court decided that the children's education was not "separate but equal" as claimed by supporters of separate schools. | In the 1950s, African-American and European-American children were often sent to separate schools in some parts of the United States. Many people who supported this segregation believed that the children were getting the same education, but the U.S. Supreme Court ruled that this was not the case in its landmark decision on *Brown vs. Board of Education* in 1954. |
| 3. The science of complexity is a study in which the relationships of elements, no matter how small, are analyzed to show how they organize to affect larger events. Complexity can be used to analyze how structures work in economy, biology, and countless other fields of study. | Complexity studies the relationship of elements to show they become organized to affect larger events. Complexity is studied in fields such as economics, biology, and others. |

Which passage is the best example of a paraphrase?

Why? _____

_____

---

### ◎ Avoiding Plagiarism

**_Rule 2: Give credit to others when you use their ideas._**

Although it is important to develop your own ideas, it is expected that you will develop those ideas based on things that other people have said or done. You may use others' ideas or quotations to support your ideas, but you must give them credit by citing the source.

- Use quotation marks for everything that comes directly from another person.

- Cite the source where you found information that is not common knowledge.

## EXERCISE 3

*Practice avoiding plagiarism by rephrasing the following passage. Read the passage one to three times, turn the page, and write your paraphrased passage without looking at the original.*

Recently, it seems that people have been forgetting their manners. It seems that people constantly answer their phones and talk during movies. However, if we look back in history, theater manners would probably be considered much worse in the past. In theaters in Europe during past centuries, fruits and vegetables were often sold as snacks instead of the popcorn, soda, and candy bars that are sold in modern theaters. If the audience didn't like what they saw in a play or other performance, they often threw their fruits and vegetables at the performers.

One of the basic and most common ways of citing sources is to write the author's name and page number after the section you have cited. Then, include the information about each source (author, title, date of publication, etc.) in a list of the works you used following your research.

### *Example:*

The following appeared in a book by an author named Belinda Briggs:

(page 27)

While Yogi Berra (former New York Yankees player and manager) said some things that may have seemed obvious or even unintelligent, there was actually a Zen quality to some of his great quotes. Perhaps this is why he is still quoted today.

For your research, you could write:

> Some of Yogi Berra's quotes had a "Zen quality" to them that has made them timeless (Briggs, 27).

You would put Briggs' words, "Zen quality," in quotations to show that they weren't your words. You would also cite the author and page number where you found the quote.

## EXERCISE 4

*Paraphrase and cite the following passages. You may quote parts (but not all) of the passages.*

1. On page 45 of a text called *World War II and the Holocaust* by Benjamin Wiley, you found the following passage:

   > Concentration camps were established across Europe during World War II in an effort to cleanse Nazi-controlled Europe of elements Hitler deemed impure, including Jews and other minorities. In some areas of Europe, Hitler's goal of ethnic cleansing was nearly successful. The Jewish population of Poland, for example, was almost entirely eliminated.

2. Paraphrase and cite the following passage by an author named Joey Joseph on page 117 of his book, *Eating Out*:

More and more Americans are eating out at restaurants. Mothers are forgetting, or in some cases, never learning to cook. American children are growing up believing that a meal is not complete without french fries. This lack of home cooking is just one of the many reasons that Americans are growing fatter and fatter.

---

### √ Tip: Citing Sources

There are several different ways of citing sources. The style you should use for citing may depend on the field of study in which you are conducting your research. Modern Language Association (MLA), Chicago Style, and American Psychological Association (APA) are a few of these styles. MLA is often used in Liberal Arts. Chicago style is used in both Liberal Arts and science. APA is often used in psychological studies and social sciences. All of these organizations publish style books and have websites to help you. Ask your instructor what style (s)he would like you to use.

**EXERCISE 5**

*Put a check next to each sentence that would be factual common knowledge.*

1. _____ Antarctica is the least populated continent in the world.

2. _____ There should not be a separation between church and state in the United States.

3. _____ Neil Armstrong became the first human to land on the moon in 1969.

4. _____ It is likely that humans will set foot on Mars before 2025.

5. _____ Jack the Ripper was probably English royalty, but it is doubtful that we will ever know for sure.

## ✓ Tip: Understanding Common Knowledge

You do not need to cite your sources for common knowledge. Common knowledge is information that is widely known by many people.

*Example:* George Washington was the first president of the United States.

To determine if something is common knowledge, check three different sources. If the information is the same in the three sources, you don't have to cite your source.

# Review—Practicing Skills from Part 4

## ▼ Using What You Have Learned

You have been given a topic in a class to compare the concepts of *nature vs. nurture* in the development of one's personality.

### EXERCISE 1: CONTEXT BUILDING

*Write what you know about the concepts of nature and nurture.*

_____

_____

_____

_____

_____

_____

## EXERCISE 2: RESEARCHING INFORMATION IN THE LIBRARY CATALOG

*There are many books written on the comparison of these subjects. It may be helpful to start with those books. Search for books in your library's online catalog **written about** nature and nurture. Complete the following chart with the information you found.*

| Author | Title | Subject | Call Number |
|--------|-------|---------|-------------|
|        |       |         |             |
|        |       |         |             |
|        |       |         |             |
|        |       |         |             |
|        |       |         |             |
|        |       |         |             |

What kind of search did you use to find books comparing nature and nurture?

_____

_____

## EXERCISE 3: RESEARCHING INFORMATION ON THE INTERNET

*Next, search for some information on the Internet about these subjects. Choose at least three websites on nature and at least three websites on nurture. Choose the sites that appear to be the most reliable and helpful for you in your research. Complete the following chart with the information you found.*

| Website | URL | Subject | Last Date Website Was Updated |
|---|---|---|---|
|  |  |  |  |
|  |  |  |  |
|  |  |  |  |
|  |  |  |  |
|  |  |  |  |
|  |  |  |  |

What did you enter for your search on these subjects?

_____

_____

## EXERCISE 4: PARAPHRASING

*A.* *Now that you have found several sources, check out one book from your list on nature vs. nurture and access one website. Find information about the arguments supporting each of these views. (Hint: You may want to look in the books' indexes under "Arguments for" or include this in your web search.)*

*Using the information you have found,* **copy** *a paragraph that you believe summarizes the evidence supporting each view.*

Support for the view that **nature** determines one's personality:

_____

_____

_____

_____

_____

_____

_____

_____

**Source:**

_____

_____

Support for the view that **nurture** determines one's
personality:

_____

_____

_____

_____

_____

_____

_____

**Source:**

_____

_____

_B. Now, read the paragraph you copied on_ nature. _Without looking at it
closely, use your own words to_ **paraphrase** _the paragraph you copied._

_____

_____

_____

_____

_____

_____

_____

*C. Give your copied paragraph and your paraphrased paragraph to your teacher or one of your classmates to read. What did he or she say about your paraphrasing?*

1. Was it too similar to the original?

2. Did you use any of the same sentences or expressions?

3. Was the information accurate and paraphrased well?

4. Do you need to cite your source in any places where the information is too similar?

**D.** *Make any necessary corrections based on this feedback so your paraphrased paragraph isn't plagiarized. Use quotation marks and cite your source if you must.*

**E.** *Now, read the paragraph you copied on* nurture. *Turn to this page and, without looking at it closely, use your own words to* **paraphrase** *the paragraph you copied.*

_____

_____

_____

_____

_____

_____

_____

*F. Once again, give your paragraphs to your teacher or to a different class-mate to read. What did he or she say about your paraphrasing?*

    1. Was it too similar to the original?

    2. Did you use any of the same sentences or expressions?

    3. Was the information accurate and paraphrased well?

    4. Do you need to cite your source in any places where the information is too similar?

*G. Again, make any necessary corrections based on this feedback so your paraphrased paragraph isn't plagiarized. Use quotation marks and cite your source if you must.*

# Comprehensive Review— Practicing Skills from All Parts

---

## ▼ Using What You Have Learned

---

The best way to practice what you have learned in this book is to practice researching a topic.

## EXERCISE 1: CHOOSING YOUR TOPIC

*Choose one of the following topics to research.*

1. **United States immigration.** Research how many people have immigrated to the United States, and at what times in history most people came to the United States. Determine which group(s) make up the largest number of immigrants in U.S. history.

2. **The history of a country of your choice.** Narrow your research to major events that have occurred in that country.

3. **A serious medical problem such as a disease, illness, or birth defect.** You may research a problem that has

been solved or a problem that still exists. Determine where and when the problem started and which people it has affected.

4. The effects of pollution on our planet. Choose one aspect of the environment such as a certain geographical location or a certain area of pollution such as water pollution. Determine what causes most of the pollution, what has been done to reduce this pollution, and what still needs to be done.

## EXERCISE 2: FINDING SOURCES

*Find your sources. Using the library catalog and/or the Internet, make a list of the sources you will use. Use no less than three sources. Alphabetize your sources by the authors' last names or by the site name.*

| Author/ Website | Title/URL | Subject | Call Number (for Books) |
|---|---|---|---|
|  |  |  |  |
|  |  |  |  |
|  |  |  |  |
|  |  |  |  |

## EXERCISE 3: SKIMMING/SCANNING TIME LINE

*Skim and scan your sources to find information for a time line. Write the important information on the time line.*

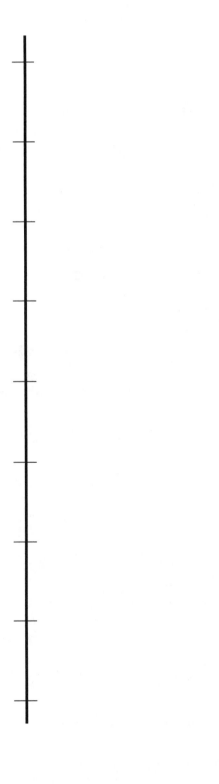

## EXERCISE 4: ORGANIZING INFORMATION

*Organize the important information from your sources in an outline, mind map, or other organizational tool. Use the space below to organize your notes.*

## EXERCISE 5: PARAPHRASING

*Without plagiarizing, paraphrase the information you have found to create a detailed outline of your research. Cite any sources and use quotation marks around any direct information you cite.*

## EXERCISE 6: WRITE YOUR RESEARCH PAPER

*Now, write your research paper, and submit it to your teacher.*

# Appendix A
## State Abbreviations

| State | Abbreviation | State | Abbreviation |
|-------|--------------|-------|--------------|
| Alabama | AL | Montana | MT |
| Alaska | AK | Nebraska | NE |
| Arizona | AZ | Nevada | NV |
| Arkansas | AR | New Hampshire | NH |
| California | CA | New Jersey | NJ |
| Colorado | CO | New Mexico | NM |
| Connecticut | CT | New York | NY |
| Delaware | DE | North Carolina | NC |
| District of Columbia | DC | North Dakota | ND |
| Florida | FL | Ohio | OH |
| Georgia | GA | Oklahoma | OK |
| Hawaii | HI | Oregon | OR |
| Idaho | ID | Pennsylvania | PA |
| Illinois | IL | Rhode Island | RI |
| Indiana | IN | South Carolina | SC |
| Iowa | IA | South Dakota | SD |
| Kansas | KS | Tennessee | TN |
| Kentucky | KY | Texas | TX |
| Louisiana | LA | Utah | UT |
| Maine | ME | Vermont | VT |
| Maryland | MD | Virginia | VA |
| Massachusetts | MA | Washington | WA |
| Michigan | MI | West Virginia | WV |
| Minnesota | MN | Wisconsin | WI |
| Mississippi | MS | Wyoming | WY |
| Missouri | MO | | |

# Appendix B
## Abbreviations for Geographical and Directional Terms

| Geographical Term | Abbreviation | Example |
| --- | --- | --- |
| archipelago | arch. | Hawaiian Arch. |
| avenue | ave. | Fifth Ave. |
| county | co. | Kent Co., Michigan |
| creek | cr. | Thompson Cr. |
| district | dist. | the Dist. of Columbia |
| drive | dr. | Binghampton Dr. |
| east | E or E. | 12 miles to the E; E. Lansing |
| elevation | elev. | elev. 7,504 feet |
| highway | hwy. | Hwy. 127 |
| island (s) | isl. | Mackinac Isl. |
| lake | L. | L. Tahoe, Nevada |
| latitude | lat. | 45° N. latitude |
| longitude | long. | 105° W. longitude |
| mount, mountain | mt. | Mt. Rainier, Grandfather Mt. |
| mountains | mts. | Rocky Mts. |
| north | N or N. | 5 miles N; N. Dakota |
| northeast | NE or N.E. | NE Asia; Garfield Street, N.E. |
| northwest | NW or N.W. | a NW wind; Pennsylvania Ave., N.W. |
| peninsula | pen. or penin. | the Malay Pen. or the Malay Penin. |
| point | pt. | Montauk Pt., New York |
| province | prov. | Quebec Prov. |
| range | ra. | the Wasatch Ra. |
| road | rd. | Cornell Rd. |
| river | r. or riv. | the Missouri R. or the Missouri Riv. |

| Geographical Term | Abbreviation | Example |
|---|---|---|
| sound | sd. | Puget Sd. |
| south | S or S. | winds S at 12 mph; S. America |
| southeast | SE or S.E. | SE Michigan; Portland St., S.E. |
| southwest | SW or S.W. | SW Asia; the S.W. suburbs |
| strait(s) | str. | the Strait of Malacca |
| territory | terr. | the Yukon Terr. |
| valley | v. or val. | the San Fernando V. or the San Fernando Val. |
| volcano | vol. | the Tararonga Vol. |
| west | W or W. | Hwy 94 W; W. Virginia |

# Appendix C
Proofreading Symbols and Abbreviations

---

## ▼ Common Proofreading Symbols

---

| Symbol | Meaning | Example |
|--------|---------|---------|
| ⌃ | insert a comma | The mayor's brother, I tell you, is a crook. |
| ⌄ | apostrophe or single quotation mark | I wouldn't know where to put this base. |
| ∧ | insert something | I know it, in fact, everyone knows it.   ; |
| ⌄⌄ ⌄⌄ | use double quotation marks | My favorite poem is Design. |
| ⊙ | use a period here | This is a declarative sentence⊙ |
| ℓ | delete | The elephant's trunk is is really its nose. |
| ∼ | transpose elements | He only picked the ones he likes. |
| ‿ | close up this space | Jordan lost his favorite basket ball. |
| # | a space needed here | I have only three friends: Ted, Raoul, and Alice. |
| ¶ | begin new paragraph | "I knew it," I said. "I thought so," she replied. |
| No ¶ | no paragraph | I knew it, she said. No ¶ "He's no good." |

**178**

# ▼ Common Proofreading Abbreviations

The abbreviation would appear in the margin, probably with a line or arrow pointing to the offending element.

| Abbreviation | Meaning | Example |
|---|---|---|
| **Ab** | a faulty abbreviation | She had earned a Phd along with her M.D. |
| **Agr**<br>See also P/A and S/V | agreement problem: subject/verb *or* pronoun/antecedent | The piano as well as the guitar need tuning.<br>The student lost their book. |
| **Awk** | awkward expression or construction | The storm had the effect of causing millions of dollars in damage. |
| **Cap** | faulty capitalization | We spent the Fall in Southern france. |
| **CS** | comma splice | Ricardo tried his best, this time that wasn't good enough |
| **DICT** | faulty diction | Due to the fact that we were wondering as to whether it would rain, we stayed home. |
| **Dgl** | dangling construction | Working harder than ever, this job proved to be too much for him to handle. |
| **- ed** | problem with final *-ed* | Last summer he walk all the way to Boston. |
| **Frag** | fragment | Depending on the amount of snow we get this winter and whether the towns buy new trucks. |
| **‖** | problem in parallel form | My car is bigger than my wife. |
| **P/A** | pronoun/antecedent agreement | A student in accounting would be wise to see their advisor this month. |

| Abbreviation | Meaning | Example |
|---|---|---|
| **Pron** | problem with pronoun | My aunt and my mother have wrecked her car<br>The committee has lost their chance to change things.<br>You'll have to do this on one's own time. |
| **Rep** | unnecessary repetition | The car was green in color. |
| **R-O** | run-on sentence | Ricardo tried his best this time that wasn't good enough. |
| **Sp** | spelling error | This sentence is flaude with two mispellings. |
| **- s** | problem with final -*s* | He wonder what these teacher think of him. |
| **STET** | Let it stand. | The proofreader uses this Latin term to indicate that proofreading marks calling for a change should be ignored and the text as originally written should be "let stand." |
| **S/V** | subject/verb agreement | The problem with these cities are leadership. |
| **T** | verb tense problem | He comes into the room, and he pulled his gun. |
| **Wdy** | wordy | Seldom have we perused a document so verbose,so ostentatious in phrasing, so burdened with too many words. |
| **WW** | wrong word | What affect did the movie have on Samantha?<br>She tried to hard to analyze its conclusion. |

# Appendix D
## Temperature Conversion

Fahrenheit

```
-40            0         32 40          80         120
 |             |          |  |           |           |
 |             |          |  |           |           |
-40          -20          0             20          40
```

Celsius

To convert a Fahrenheit temperature into degrees Celsius, first subtract 32 from the Fahrenheit temperature. Then multiply by five-ninths.

To convert a Celsius temperature into degrees Fahrenheit, first multiply the Celsius temperature by nine-fifths. Then add 32.

The Celsius temperature scale is still sometimes referred to as the "centigrade" scale.

# Appendix E
Weights and Measures

## ▼ Metric Units of Measurement

The prefixes for the different units of length, volume, and mass in the metric system obey the following rules:

| Prefix | Multiply by |
|--------|-------------|
| milli- | 0.001 |
| centi- | 0.01 |
| deci- | 0.1 |
| deka- | 10 |
| hecto- | 100 |
| kilo- | 1000 |

## ▽ LENGTH

The standard unit of length in the metric system is the meter. Other units of length and their equivalents in meters are as follows:

| 1 millimeter (mm) | = 0.001 meter (m) |
|-------------------|-------------------|
| 1 centimeter (cm) | = 0.01 meter |
| 1 decimeter (dm) | = 0.1 meter |
| 1 kilometer (km) | = 1,000 meters |

## ▽ VOLUME

The standard unit of volume in the metric system is the liter. One liter is equal to 1,000 cubic centimeters in volume. Other units of volume and their equivalents in liters are as follows:

| 1 milliliter (ml) | = 0.001 liter (l) |
|---|---|
| 1 centiliter (cl) | = 0.01 liter |
| 1 deciliter (dl) | = 0.1 liter |
| 1 kiloliter (kl) | = 1,000 liters |

## ▽ WEIGHT

The standard unit of weight in the metric system is the gram. Other units of weight and their equivalents in grams are as follows:

| 1 milligram (mg) | = 0.001 gram (g) |
|---|---|
| 1 centigram (cg) | = 0.01 gram |
| 1 decigram (dg) | = 0.1 gram |
| 1 kilogram (kg) | = 1,000 grams |

# ▼ U.S. System of Measurement

## ▽ LENGTH

| | |
|---|---|
| 12 inches (in.) | = 1 foot (ft.) |
| 3 feet | = 1 yard (yd.) |
| 5,280 feet | = 1 mile (mi.) |
| 1,760 yards | = 1 mile (mi.) |

## ▽ AREA

| | |
|---|---|
| 144 square inches (sq. in.) ($in^2$) | = 1 square foot (sq. ft.)($ft^2$) |
| 9 square feet | = 1 square yard ($yd^2$) |
| 4,840 square yards | = 1 acre |
| 640 acres | = 1 square mile ($mi^2$) |
| 1 square mile | = 1 section |
| 36 sections | = 1 township |

## ▽ VOLUME

| | |
|---|---|
| 1,728 cubic inches ($in^3$) | = 1 cubic foot ($ft^3$) |
| 27 cubic feet | = 1 cubic yard ($yd^3$) |

## ▽ CAPACITY (Dry)

| 2 pints (pt.) | = 1 quart (qt.) |
|---|---|
| 8 quarts | = 1 peck (pk.) |
| 4 pecks | = 1 bushel (bu.) |

## ▽ CAPACITY (LIQUID)

| 16 fluid ounces (fl. oz.) | = 1 pint (pt.) |
|---|---|
| 2 pints | = 1 quart (qt.) |
| 4 quarts | = 1 gallon (gal.) |

## ▽ WEIGHT

| 16 ounces (oz.) | = 1 pound (lb.) |
|---|---|
| 2,000 pounds | = 1 ton |

# Answer Key

## Part 1: Organizing Information (pages 1–48)

### LESSON 1: Alphabetizing (pages 3–10)

#### Exercise 1 (page 5)

| | |
|---|---|
| quadrant | 2 |
| quadrilateral | 3 |
| parallelogram | 1 |
| | |
| pianissimo | 2 |
| staccato | 4 |
| pizzicato | 3 |
| allegro | 1 |
| | |
| attack | 1 |
| blitzkrieg | 2 |
| surrender | 4 |
| invasion | 3 |
| | |
| solution | 5 |
| element | 2 |
| atom | 1 |
| mixture | 3 |
| nucleus | 4 |

#### Exercise 2 (page 5)

1. *colony*
2. freedom
3. persecution
4. pilgrim
5. settlement
6. settlers

#### Exercise 3 (page 6)

1. *César Chávez*
2. Medgar Evers
3. Jesse Jackson
4. Martin Luther King, Jr.
5. Rosa Parks

#### Exercise 4 (page 8)

Word meanings may vary. The words are placed in alphabetical order below, with one possible meaning each.

1. astronaut: an American space traveler
2. cosmonaut: a Russian space traveler
3. interplanetary probe: a ship sent to another planet
4. orbit: travel around something
5. satellite: an object put into space that circles a planet
6. space race: the U.S. and Russian competition to be first in various forms of space exploration
7. suborbital trip: less than a complete orbit

### Alphabetizing Names from Reading Passages for Study Purposes (page 9)

In 1926, (Robert Goddard) launched the first liquid fuel rocket in the United States. However, it wasn't until 1957 that the first satellite was launched into orbit by the Soviet Union. In 1959, (Yuri Gagarin,) a Russian cosmonaut, became the first human being to go into space and orbit the Earth. In the same year, the Russians also launched the first interplanetary probe to Venus. The U.S. sent its first astronaut, (Alan B. Shepard,) into space in 1961. Shepard's trip was a suborbital trip. A year later, astronaut (John Herschel Glenn, Jr.) became the first U.S. astronaut to orbit the Earth, three years after Gagarin. The Russian space program achieved another first by sending (Valentina Vladimirovna Tereshkova) into orbit in 1963. Tereshkova was a female cosmonaut and was thus the first woman to go into space. The Russians and Americans continued the space race throughout the 1960s, until the U.S. landed the first humans on another body in orbit in 1969. (Neil Armstrong) and (Edwin "Buzz" Aldrin,) U.S. astronauts in the Apollo 11 mission, became the first humans to walk on the Moon in July 1969.

## Exercise 5 (page 10)

1. Edwin "Buzz" Aldrin: the second human to walk on the Moon
2. Neil Armstrong: the first human to walk on the Moon
3. Yuri Gagarin: the first human being in space
4. John Herschel Glenn, Jr.: the first American to orbit the Earth
5. Robert Goddard: the first person to launch a liquid fuel rocket
6. Alan B. Shepard: the first U.S. astronaut sent into space
7. Valentina Vladimirovna Tereshkova: the first woman to go into space

## LESSON 2: Making and Interpreting Time Lines (pages 11–20)

### Exercise 1 (page 12)

1. The Life of John F. Kennedy
2. Kennedy was born in Massachusetts in 1917.
3. Kennedy was killed in Dallas, Texas, in 1963.
4. Kennedy was elected President of the U.S. in 1961.
5. Kennedy was killed in 1963.

### Exercise 2 (page 14)

Answers will vary.

### Exercise 3 (page 15)

Answers will vary.

### Exercise 4 (page 17)

1. 8
2. Hawaii
3. August 21, 1959
4. 2
5. 0
6. 2

7. 46 (almost 47)
8. Idaho/Wyoming, New Mexico/Arizona, Alaska/Hawaii
9. They became states in the same years.
10. Many years passed between the time that Arizona and Alaska became states.

### Exercise 5 (page 18)

Important Soviet Events during World War II

| | |
|---|---|
| 1939 | The Soviet Union agreed to split Poland with Germany after Germany invaded Poland and began World War II. |
| 1940 | |
| 1941 | The German army invaded the Soviet Union without warning. |
| 1942 | |
| 1943 | German troops at Stalingrad surrender. |
| 1944 | The Soviet Union drove the German army from Pskov, the last large Russian city. |
| 1945 | The Soviet Union's leader Joseph Stalin met with British and American leaders to discuss how to divide Europe after the war. |

### Exercise 6 (page 20)

1. The Soviet Union agreed to split Poland with Germany after Germany invaded Poland and began World War II
2. 1939
3. 1945
4. 1939–1945
5. 1944
6. No
7. Explanations for item 5 will vary. One possible answer: *At the beginning of the war, Germany had agreed to give some of its conquered land to the Soviet Union.*

## LESSON 3: Outlining (pages 21–28)

### Exercise 1 (page 23)

**First-level (boxed):** raising money for the government, a tool for influencing spending behavior, an instrument of industrial strategy, a means of advancing moral policy

**Second-level (circled):** charitable-deduction rule, mortgage interest deduction

**Third-level:** None

## Exercise 2 (page 24)

### *The Use of U. S. Tax Policy*

> I. Raise money for the government
> II. Influence spending behavior
>   a. charitable deduction rule
>   b. mortgage interest deduction
> III. Industrial strategy (e.g., tax credits for ethanol)
> IV. Moral policy (e.g., stem-cell research)

## Exercise 3: Critical Thinking (page 25)

Answers will vary. One possible list:

### Characteristics of a Good Outline

1. Only main points go in an outline.
2. Points are not whole sentences.
3. It doesn't make a new level for only one point of support; a single point might be listed as an example in the next highest level.
4. If other people will read it, it should use the system of Roman numerals, letters, and Arabic numerals.
5. The main idea of the whole reading or lecture is listed as a title, not as a level-one point.

## Exercise 4 (page 27)

Answers will vary. One possible way of categorizing the points is given below. Points marked "YES" are <u>almost certainly important</u> in a speech on the topic. Points marked "MAYBE" might be useful but <u>could be deleted</u> if you don't have time for them. Points marked "NO" should probably not be used because they <u>don't strongly relate the topic</u>. Points marked "NEW" are all <u>useful points found through further research</u>.

- underground water picks up different pollutants from above-ground water—oil, gas, manure, sewage, chemicals **YES**
- as water flows through sand or stone, some impurities are filtered out  **MAYBE**
- bad to mix sewage systems from homes with storm runoff  **MAYBE**
- filters can be installed in homes **NO** (This presentation should concentrate on describing a situation, not on correcting a problem. You have only 5 minutes, so you can't cover everything.)
- public water sources should be inspected **NO** (This presentation should concentrate on describing a situation, not on correcting a problem. You have only 5 minutes, so you can't cover everything.)
- factories: what are they putting into water? **YES**
- living bacteria or algae can make you sick **MAYBE**
- waste from animals or humans **MAYBE**

## LESSON 4: Other Shortcuts for Organizing Information (pages 29–39)

### Exercise 1: Critical Thinking (page 33)

Answers will vary. Some possible answers:

**Advantages of Using Marginal Notes**

- Don't have to rewrite words that are already printed
- Can use arrows
- Can use abbreviations
- Don't have to re-organize notes
- Notes and reading are together in one place

**Disadvantages of Using Marginal Notes**

- Sometimes margins are thin and you can't write much
- Only useful for readings you can write on
- If you lose the reading you also lose your notes

### Exercise 2 (page 34)

Answers will vary. One possible set of notes:

---

*Cher.*
*Ind. were*
*the victims*

**The Trail of Tears**

*What was the*
*problem?*

To the American government, it became obvious after the Louisiana Purchase (1803) that the "Indian Problem" in the Southeast should involve shipping Indians West. These included the Cherokee (who call themselves the Ani Yun Wiya).

The Cherokees had developed a civilization that whites had to respect. *highly cultured* Their system of Civil Law was advanced, and they had a written language—in their own, unique characters, not just an English-letter transliteration. *? check meaning ?*

*real reason*
*for whites* →

Once gold was discovered under Cherokee land in Georgia, the federal

*legal*
*justification*

Indian Removal Act of 1830 sealed the Cherokees' fate.

About 16,000 Cherokees, divided into 16 units, were assembled under *1,000 per unit*

*was he*
*president*
*then?*

Andrew Jackson's generals and headed west, toward what is now Oklahoma. *check map!* Some traveled on the Arkansas River, which was full of debris and ice from spring melt-off. Others traveled by land across roadless territory with few clean *branches, etc? dangerous?* sources of water. Altogether about 8,000 Cherokees died along what has become known as the Trail of Tears. = 50%!

---

## Exercise 3 (page 36)

therefore, b

something, g

more than, h

according to Johnson, f

United Nations, i

about, approximately, e

forbidden, c

later on, d

three distribution systems, a

## Exercise 4 (page 36)

Answers will vary. One possible list:

1. long words get chopped off ("dist sys")

2. use initials

3. sometimes use symbols (like = or >) instead of words

4. each note-taker can make up his or her own system

5. enable you to write more notes in a margin

6. grammar not necessary to show relationships; arrows or other symbols can do it instead

## Exercise 5 (page 37)

Answers will vary. Some possible abbreviations:

| Notes in Full Form | Your Abbreviation |
| --- | --- |
| Shakespeare's romantic plays are perfect examples of the English Renaissance. | S. plays = good e.g. Eng. Ren. |
| A package sent via the National Postal Service costs three cents per pound less than the next-cheapest service. | NPS rate = 3 ¢/ lb < other chpst |
| Sir Nigel Watson fought Madame Gemma Stykes for leadership of the Worker's Party. | NG vs. GS for head, WP |
| Upper respiratory infections become common in the winter not because of cold but because more people are gathered indoors for a long time. | Winter URI (e.g. colds) ← people together indoors not ← temp. |

### LESSON 5: Review—Practicing Skills from Part 1 (pages 40–48)

### Exercise 1: Alphabetizing (page 45)

1. John Adams
2. Aaron Burr
3. Benjamin Franklin
4. Alexander Hamilton
5. Thomas Jefferson
6. James Madison
7. James Monroe
8. George Washington

### Exercise 2: Timeline (page 46)

about 1760 American colonists started to become angry about British taxes.

1774 The First Continental Congress met to issue a list of items that angered them to the King of England.

1775 The Revolutionary War began. Washington was put in charge of the troops.

1776 Thomas Jefferson wrote the draft of the Declaration of Independence.

1777 The Articles of Confederation are drafted by the Continental Congress

1781 The Revolutionary War ended.

1789 George Washington was elected the first President of the United States.

1791 The Bill of Rights was added to the new Constitution.

1797 John Adams became President.

1801 Thomas Jefferson became President.

1809 James Madison became President

1817 James Monroe became President

### Exercise 3 (page 47)

Answers will vary.

### Exercise 4 (page 48)

Answers will vary.

## Part 2: Reading and Interpreting Illustrated Information (pages 49–82)

### LESSON 6: Reading and Interpreting Maps (pages 51–58)

### Exercise 1 (page 52)

1. *The Continental United States*
2. It shows the 48 connected states in the U.S.
3. It shows the shape of the United States and its continental states.

### Exercise 2 (page 53)

1. It shows the United States.

2. It provides information on population change in all the states.

3. The key shows how a color indicates the percentage of population change.

4. The U.S. Census Bureau created the map.

### Exercise 3 (page 54)

1. b

2. a

3. d

4. c

5. a

### Exercise 4 (page 56)

1. It addresses Japan's population.

2. Japan is the tenth most populous country.

3. Japan is the 62nd largest country in the world.

4. No

5. It shows where people live in Japan.

6. Most people live in the middle and south parts of Honshu in the crowded metropolitan areas near the sea.

7. Most of the interior of the central island, Honshu, is covered with mountains where people cannot live.

## LESSON 7: Reading and Interpreting Graphs (pages 59–66)

### Exercise 1 (page 60)

1. It provides information on immigration to the U.S. from 1820 to 2010.

2. The numbers show the number of people who immigrated to the U.S.

3. The numbers show specific years.

4. b

5. c

### Exercise 2 (page 62)

1. The bars on the graph point to the side, not up.

2. Answers may vary. (Example: Growing occupations)

3. The names of the jobs are presented on the vertical axis.

4. The number of jobs (in thousands) is presented on the horizontal axis.

5. Answers may vary. (Example: Registered nurse)

6. d

7. c

### Exercise 3 (page 64)

1. Accidents increased between 1990 and 2000. In 1990, there were only about 30 accidents, but in 2000, there were about 70 accidents.

2. Accidents will continue to increase if nothing changes.

3. Answers may vary. (Example: Pass news laws that make the roads safer.)

## Exercise 4 (page 65)

1. The graph shows world population growth throughout history.

2. The numbers represent billions of people.

3. The numbers represent years.

4. World population increased dramatically in the Modern Age.

5. Answers may vary. (Example: *It means that there are more people in the world than there ever were.*)

6. Answers may vary. (Example: *There will not be enough food to feed everyone.*)

## LESSON 8: Reading and Interpreting Charts and Tables (pages 67–75)

### Exercise 1 (page 68)

1. Most people voted for the Democratic Party.

2. The fewest people voted for the Independent Party.

3. b

### Exercise 2 (page 69)

The answer is discussed on page 70.

### Exercise 3 (page 70)

b, c, d, e, g

### Exercise 4 (page 71)

Answers may vary because questions ask for personal interpretations, but the best answers are:

1. No

2. No

3. No. The table does not show that the temperatures in Chicago are getting warmer every year.

### Exercise 5 (page 73)

1. The Labour Party won the most seats.

2. The UK Unionists and Independent parties won the fewest seats.

3. The table is organized by the percentage of votes for each party. The first party in the table has the largest percentage.

4. The Labour Party seems to have had the largest influence in the Parliament because it had more seats than all the other parties combined.

5. The Conservative Party lost the most seats. The Labour Party won the most seats, so the Labour Party probably became much stronger than the Conservative Party.

## LESSON 9: Review—Practicing Skills from Part 2 (pages 76–82)

### Exercise 1: Tables (page 76)

1. The table shows the number and size of earthquakes in the U.S. from 2000–2003 and the number of people who died in those earthquakes.
2. Yes
3. No
4. Yes
5. Answers may vary. (Example: You could use the numbers of total earthquakes.)

### Exercise 2: Graphs (page 78)

1. The graph shows the number of earthquakes in the U.S. compared to the number of earthquakes in the world from 2000–2003.
2. Yes
3. No
4. Answers may vary. (Example: *New technology helps scientists detect earthquakes better than in the past.*)
5. You could use the total number of earthquakes in the world.

### Exercise 3: Maps (page 80)

1. It is located on the North American Plate.
2. The Caribbean Plate, the Cocos Plate, the Pacific Plate, and the Juan De Fuca Plate all touch the North American Plate.
3. They touch near California, Oregon, Washington, and Alaska.
4. California, Oregon, Washington, and Alaska
5. Answers will vary. (Example: It shows where earthquakes may occur.)

### Exercise 4: Pie Chart (page 81)

1. California
2. The Pacific Plate rubs against the North American Plate near California and causes many earthquakes.
3. Answers will vary. (Example: You could use the information on which state has the most earthquakes.)

### Exercise 5: Consolidating Information (page 82)

1. Answers will vary. (Example: You could write about why California has so many earthquakes.)
2. Answers will vary. (Example: You may need to find out what size earthquakes California has.)

## *Part 3: Skills for Better Reading (pages 83–142)*

## LESSON 10: Determining the Main Idea (pages 85–98)

### Exercise 1 (page 88)

1. The reading says that the *structure* of feathers provides *insulation* for a bird.
2. *pockets of air*; maintain its body temperature; air pockets; insulation
3. The structural features of a feather are a key element in helping the animal maintain its body temperature.

### Exercise 2 (page 90)

| | |
|---|---|
| 1. T | 5. T |
| 2. T | 6. T |
| 3. S | 7. T |
| 4. T | 8. T |

### Exercise 3 (page 91)

Answers will vary. One possible answer: Sentence 7 and sentence 8 state simple, obvious facts that would be hard to develop into a meaningful essay. Sentence 7 allows some development (more than does sentence 8), but not enough to fill an entire essay.

### Exercise 4 (page 91)

1. The main idea of the reading is that glaciers shaped the land of southwestern Minnesota and eastern South Dakota.
2. The two sentences that do not fit in with this main idea are: *(a) Today, this region is governed partly by the states of Minnesota and South Dakota and partly by the Sisseton Band of the Lakota. (b) The craters, or caldera, of volcanoes also often form lakes.*
3. a. glacial moraine; b. pothole lakes; c. drift soil

### Exercise 5 (page 94)

1. b
2. *this insect, it, exotic species, the bug, the borer, this copper-colored beetle, its*

### Exercise 6 (page 96)

1. Answers will vary. One possible answer: *The author's purpose was to explain why the emerald ash borer is a serious problem.*
2. Answers will vary. One possible answer: *The author mentions other diseases because their similarities to the ash borer problem (Dutch elm disease) or their differences from it (oak wilt) help explain the seriousness of the situation.*

### Exercise 7 (page 98)

Main ideas:

1. The main economic systems now are socialism, free-market capitalism, and centralism.
2. The temperature in some upper layers of the atmosphere is very high.
3. Global warming is leading to extreme weather events.

## LESSON 11: Types of Writing on Assignments and Tests (pages 99–110)

### Exercise 1 (page 100)

| | |
|---|---|
| 1. A | 7. A |
| 2. N | 8. N or A (depending on how technical the class is; the language may be too complex for some papers) |
| 3. A (if you are good friends) | |
| 4. N | 9. N |
| 5. N | 10. A |
| 6. N | |

### Exercise 2: Discussion (page 101)

Answers will vary.

### Exercise 3 (page 102)

Answers will vary. One possible list:

- mystery novels
- essays for college applications
- biographies (books about people's lives)

### Exercise 4 (page 103)

1. an owner's manual for a product
2. an answer to a definition question on a test
3. a romance novel
4. an entry in a personal journal
5. a news report about a robbery
6. a horror story

### Exercise 5 (page 107)

1. application
2. expression of opinion (or evaluation)
3. classification
4. chronology
5. persuasion (or expression of opinion)
6. comparison / contrast
7. definition
8. narration
9. analysis (or expression of opinion)

## LESSON 12: Scanning and Skimming (pages 111–123)

### Exercise 1 (page 112)

1. 18
2. on pages v and vi
3. on pages 51–58
4. on pages 155–162
5. Appendixes A–E and an answer key

### Exercise 2 (page 113)

The wording of answers will vary. In content, the answers should be as below:

1. Links to information about the U.S. Department of State, its activities, and its publications
2. To take you quickly to one of the sections that are listed in
   detail at the left side of the page.
3. By clicking on [full text].
4. To link to stories that are not as new as those in the "Highlights" section.

### Exercise 3 (page 115)

Answers will vary. One possible list:

the time of a movie

a friend's address in an address book

a telephone number

the score of a game described in a sports article

the name of the author of an article

the total amount you must pay, according to a bill

things you must do today, according to a calendar

### Exercise 4 (page 116)

1. Gold

2. a researcher at Dealy College

3. Thomas Fein

4. Boston

### Exercise 5 (page 118)

1. 500

2. in the 1980s

3. Dealey College

4. *Cellular Studies*

5. Boston

### Exercise 6 (page 118)

Answers may vary, which is acceptable if the student can support a variant answer. The most likely choices are Science Survivors: A High School Survival Guide; Atmospheric Structure: A Basic Guide to Inner Space; Science Encyclopedia for the Amateur. A Basic Look.

### Exercise 7: Discussion (page 120)

Answers will vary. Various choices can be excluded because they are persuasive, not factual, or they relate to some odd meaning of the term (e.g., as the name of a rock band), or because they are written for a younger audience.

### Exercise 8 (page 121)

Answers about the "clues" may vary.

1. The National Atmospheric Administration Report on the State of the Air. Clue: The site's address contains ".gov."

2. Meteorology 101. Clue: The title of the site includes the phrase "Montfortune University."

3. Bubble inside Bubble. Clue: The site's address contains ".org."

### Exercise 9: Discussion (page 122)

Answers may vary slightly.

1. bubonic plague (also rats or disease)

2. Promontory, Utah (also Union Pacific or Central Pacific)

3. psyche and Freud

## LESSON 13: Vocabulary Strategies (pages 124–142)

### Exercise 1 (page 126)

1. nc 3
2. product—4
3. paint—vt 1
4. shelf—2
5. product—2

6. paint—nc
7. product—2
8. studying—vt, 2
9. paint—nu 1
10. study—nu

### Exercise 2 (page 128)

1. a
2. b
3. b
4. d
5. c

6. c
7. c
8. c
9. a
10. a

### Exercise 3: Critical Thinking (page 133)
Answers will vary.

## LESSON 14: Review—Practicing Skills from Part 3 (pages 137–142)

1. b
2. a
3. d
4. b
5. a
6. a
7. c

8. c
9. a
10. d
11. b
12. a
13. a
14. d

## *Part 4: Research Strategies (pages 143–174)*

## LESSON 15:  Finding Information for Research (pages 145–154)
All exercises: Answers will vary.

## LESSON 16:  Avoiding Plagiarism (pages 155–162)

### Exercise 2 (page 156)
The second passage is paraphrased best. The paraphrase gives the same information, but states it much differently than the original passage.

### Exercise 3 (page 159)
Answers will vary.

### Exercise 4 (page 160)
Answers will vary.

**Exercise 5 (page 162)**

Check items 1 and 3.

**LESSON 17:  Review—Practicing Skills from Part 4 (pages 163–169)**

All exercises: Answers will vary.

**LESSON 18: Comprehensive Review—Practicing Skills from All Parts (pages 170–174)**

All exercises: Answers will vary.

# Acknowledgments

*Grateful acknowledgment is made to the following authors, publishers, and journals for permission to reprint previously published materials.*

Library of Congress, Prints and Photographs Division, for photographs of: John F. Kennedy, LC-USZ62-117124; Thomas Edison, LC-D414-K3490; and George Westinghouse, LC-USZ62-93492.

Corbis for image of Historic United States Betsy Ross Flag.

Deborah Kopka for illustrations.

Professor Michael Parsons for "British Election of 1997 Table," *http://www.univ-pau.fr/~parsons/brcivhom.html.*

Population Reference Bureau for "World Population Growth Graph," *http://www.prb.org/Content/NavigationMenu/PRB/Educators/Human_Population/Population_Growth/Population_Growth.htm.*

The Project Apollo Archive for "Aldrin Salutes U.S. Flag" image, AS11-40-5874, courtesy of NASA, scanned by Kipp Teague.

Thomson Learning for chart entitled THE FOURTEEN WORDS by I. S. P. Nation (1990), from Exploring Second Language Reading, Issues and Strategies 1st edition by ANDERSON. © 1999. Reprinted with permission of Heinle, a division of Thomson Learning: *www.thomsonrights.com.* Fax: 800-730-2215.

World Book Online Reference Center for "The Population Density Map of Japan." World Book Online Reference Center. 2004. *http://www.worldbookonline.com/wb/ExtMedia?id=ar285600&st=Japan&em=mp000356* © 2004 World Book, Inc., by permission of the publisher.

*Every effort has been made to contact the copyright holders for permission to reprint borrowed material. We regret any oversights that may have occurred and will rectify them in future printings of this book.*